OPPOSING VIEWPOINTS® SERIES

Chemical Dependency

Other Books of Related Interest:

"Congress shall make
no law . . . abridging
the freedom of speech,
or of the press."

First Amendment to the U.S. Constitution

The basic foundation of our democracy is the First Amendment guarantee of freedom of expression. The Opposing Viewpoints Series is dedicated to the concept of this basic freedom and the idea that it is more important to practice it than to enshrine it.

Chemical Dependency

Roman Espejo, Book Editor

GREENHAVEN PRESS
A part of Gale, Cengage Learning

Detroit • New York • San Francisco • New Haven, Conn • Waterville, Maine • London

GALE
CENGAGE Learning

Christine Nasso, *Publisher*
Elizabeth Des Chenes, *Managing Editor*

© 2011 Greenhaven Press, a part of Gale, Cengage Learning

For more information, contact:
Greenhaven Press
27500 Drake Rd.
Farmington Hills, MI 48331-3535
Or you can visit our Internet site at gale.cengage.com

For product information and technology assistance, contact us at

Gale Customer Support, 1-800-877-4253
For permission to use material from this text or product, submit all requests online at www.cengage.com/permissions

Further permissions questions can be emailed to permissionrequest@cengage.com

Articles in Greenhaven Press anthologies are often edited for length to meet page requirements. In addition, original titles of these works are changed to clearly present the main thesis and to explicitly indicate the author's opinion. Every effort is made to ensure that Greenhaven Press accurately reflects the original intent of the authors. Every effort has been made to trace the owners of copyrighted material.

Cover image © Laurence Mouton/és Photography/Corbis.

LIBRARY OF CONGRESS CATALOGING-IN-PUBLICATION DATA

Chemical dependency / Roman Espejo, book editor.
    p. cm. -- (Opposing viewpoints)
    Includes bibliographical references and index.
    ISBN 978-0-7377-5215-1 (hardcover) -- ISBN 978-0-7377-5216-8 (pbk.)
    1. Substance abuse--Juvenile literature. 2. Substance abuse--Treatment--Juvenile literature. I. Espejo, Roman, 1977-
    HV4998.C444 2011
    362.29--dc22
                                                            2010040829

Printed in the United States of America
1 2 3 4 5 6 7 15 14 13 12 11

Contents

Chapter 3: What Drug Treatment and Prevention Programs Are Effective?

Chapter 4: Should Drug Laws Be Changed?

Why Consider Opposing Viewpoints?

> *"The only way in which a human being can make some approach to knowing the whole of a subject is by hearing what can be said about it by persons of every variety of opinion and studying all modes in which it can be looked at by every character of mind. No wise man ever acquired his wisdom in any mode but this."*
>
> John Stuart Mill

In our media-intensive culture it is not difficult to find differing opinions. Thousands of newspapers and magazines and dozens of radio and television talk shows resound with differing points of view. The difficulty lies in deciding which opinion to agree with and which "experts" seem the most credible. The more inundated we become with differing opinions and claims, the more essential it is to hone critical reading and thinking skills to evaluate these ideas. Opposing Viewpoints books address this problem directly by presenting stimulating debates that can be used to enhance and teach these skills. The varied opinions contained in each book examine many different aspects of a single issue. While examining these conveniently edited opposing views, readers can develop critical thinking skills such as the ability to compare and contrast authors' credibility, facts, argumentation styles, use of persuasive techniques, and other stylistic tools. In short, the Opposing Viewpoints Series is an ideal way to attain the higher-level thinking and reading skills so essential in a culture of diverse and contradictory opinions.

In addition to providing a tool for critical thinking, Opposing Viewpoints books challenge readers to question their own strongly held opinions and assumptions. Most people form their opinions on the basis of upbringing, peer pressure, and personal, cultural, or professional bias. By reading carefully balanced opposing views, readers must directly confront new ideas as well as the opinions of those with whom they disagree. This is not to simplistically argue that everyone who reads opposing views will—or should—change his or her opinion. Instead, the series enhances readers' understanding of their own views by encouraging confrontation with opposing ideas. Careful examination of others' views can lead to the readers' understanding of the logical inconsistencies in their own opinions, perspective on why they hold an opinion, and the consideration of the possibility that their opinion requires further evaluation.

Evaluating Other Opinions

To ensure that this type of examination occurs, Opposing Viewpoints books present all types of opinions. Prominent spokespeople on different sides of each issue as well as well-known professionals from many disciplines challenge the reader. An additional goal of the series is to provide a forum for other, less known, or even unpopular viewpoints. The opinion of an ordinary person who has had to make the decision to cut off life support from a terminally ill relative, for example, may be just as valuable and provide just as much insight as a medical ethicist's professional opinion. The editors have two additional purposes in including these less known views. One, the editors encourage readers to respect others' opinions—even when not enhanced by professional credibility. It is only by reading or listening to and objectively evaluating others' ideas that one can determine whether they are worthy of consideration. Two, the inclusion of such viewpoints encourages the important critical thinking skill of ob-

jectively evaluating an author's credentials and bias. This evaluation will illuminate an author's reasons for taking a particular stance on an issue and will aid in readers' evaluation of the author's ideas.

It is our hope that these books will give readers a deeper understanding of the issues debated and an appreciation of the complexity of even seemingly simple issues when good and honest people disagree. This awareness is particularly important in a democratic society such as ours in which people enter into public debate to determine the common good. Those with whom one disagrees should not be regarded as enemies but rather as people whose views deserve careful examination and may shed light on one's own.

Thomas Jefferson once said that "difference of opinion leads to inquiry, and inquiry to truth." Jefferson, a broadly educated man, argued that "if a nation expects to be ignorant and free . . . it expects what never was and never will be." As individuals and as a nation, it is imperative that we consider the opinions of others and examine them with skill and discernment. The Opposing Viewpoints Series is intended to help readers achieve this goal.

David L. Bender and Bruno Leone,
Founders

Introduction

> *"Regulating marijuana will take marijuana out of the hands of criminals and put it where it belongs: in a well-regulated, licensed market only available to adults."*
>
> —*Marijuana Policy Project*

> *"Marijuana use is increasing among today's youth, and as a mother and a grandmother, I am concerned by any initiative that might contribute to increased substance abuse."*
>
> —*Lynn Woolsey,*
> *Democratic congresswoman*

In July 2010 a poll on California's Proposition 19—also known as the Regulate, Control and Tax Cannabis Act of 2010—revealed that the majority of its citizens may support the legalization of possession and cultivation of marijuana for personal use. In the poll, 49 percent approved the proposition, 41 percent disapproved it, and 10 percent were undecided. Advocates of the proposition include several police and legal officials, including San Jose chief of police Joseph McNamara, retired Los Angeles deputy chief of police Stephen Downing, and retired judge James Gray. "Outlawing marijuana hasn't stopped 100 million Americans from trying it,"[1] states their signed ballot argument. "But we can control it, make it harder for kids to get, weaken the cartels, focus police resources on violent crime, and generate billions in revenue and savings. We need a commonsense approach to control marijuana."

1. Politifi.com, "Law Enforcement for California's Prop 19," July 14, 2010. http://politifi.com.

Proposition 19 garners support on these grounds. According to a study published by the RAND Drug Policy Research Center, decriminalization would result in a drop of marijuana prices, from $375 to $38 per ounce—the cost of medical marijuana in California—and essentially level the black market for pot. "Right now, when individuals purchase drugs, they are paying for the drug dealer taking risks of being arrested,"[2] says Beau Kilmer, lead author of the study and codirector of the RAND center. Moreover, the Drug Policy Alliance (DPA) alleges that existing enforcement is racially biased in the state, insisting that African Americans use pot less than whites. "[F]rom 2004 through 2008, in every one of the twenty-five largest counties in California, blacks were arrested for marijuana possession at higher rates than whites, typically at double, triple, or even quadruple the rate of whites," the DPA study found. California National Association for the Advancement of Colored People (NAACP) president Alice Huffman agreed. "There is a strong racial component that must be considered when we investigate how the marijuana laws are applied to people of color," she claims. And a California resident published on the *Los Angeles Times' Comments Blog*, upholds that the passage of Proposition 19 would not increase marijuana use. "The number of kids who smoke pot will probably not increase because, unlike alcohol, the smell of marijuana carries and is much more difficult to conceal,"[3] the reader contends. "I think the prognostications that legalization will lead to wider use are unfounded and totally unprovable."

Beliefs and views surrounding marijuana are deeply divided, however, and Proposition 19 attracts vigorous opposition. California senator Dianne Feinstein declared her position via e-mail. "Proposition 19 is simply a jumbled legal nightmare that will make our highways, our workplaces, and our

2. Lisa Leff, "Study: Pot Prices Would Plummet with Legalization," *Salon*, July 7, 2010. www.salon.com.
3. "Orange County Legal Secretary Grows Medical Marijuana Legally, Happily," June 1, 2010. http://latimesblogs.latimes.com.

communities less safe."[4] Feinstein claims that "there are too many unknown factors related to law enforcement and public safety." Additionally, she insists that the RAND study shows that pot use will increase and California will lose federal funding. State attorney general Jerry Brown made his stance clear at the California District Attorneys Association conference in June 2010, asserting that instead of toppling them, Proposition 19 would urge Mexican drug cartels to rush into California. "Every year we get more and more marijuana,"[5] Brown says, "and every year we find more guys with AK-47s coming out of Mexico going into forests and growing more and more dangerous and losing control." Ron Allen, a prominent minister and member of the California NAACP, also attacked the association's support of the proposition in the name of racial equality. Allen claims that Alice Huffman was bribed by George Soros, a billionaire lobbyist who finances the movement to legalize pot. "With Huffman's position on legalization, she is destroying the good work the NAACP has done for the African American people, and she is discrediting the good name of the NAACP,"[6] he argues.

California voters will decide the fate of Proposition 19 in November 2010. As the most populous state in America, California's legalization of marijuana through the proposition could have ramifications on other states' policies and lawmaking. *Opposing Viewpoints: Chemical Dependency* investigates drug prohibition and other topics in the following four chapters: "Is Chemical Dependency a Serious Problem?" "What Causes Chemical Dependency?" "What Drug Treatment and Prevention Programs Are Effective?" and "Should Drug Laws Be Changed?" The balkanized and passionate assertions and

4. Robert Cruickshank, "Will the CDP Endorse Prop 19?" Calitics.com, July 13, 2010. www.calitics.com.
5. Steven Greenhut, "Can GOP Quit Weed Whacking?" *Orange County Register*, July 10, 2010. www.ocregister.com.
6. Prnewswire.com, "Minister Speaks Out Against California NAACP's Support of Proposition 19," July 1, 2010. www.prnewswire.com.

opinions of the authors in this volume—from law enforcement to scientific researchers to addiction specialists—are a testament to the enduring debates concerning drug use in America.

OPPOSING
VIEWPOINTS®
SERIES

Is Chemical Dependency a Serious Problem?

Chapter Preface

On January 23, 2006, Brett Chidester pitched a tent in his father's garage. Inside, he fired a charcoal grill and died of carbon monoxide poisoning. "How can I go on living after I learned the secrets of life,"[1] the Wilmington, Delaware, teenager wrote in his suicide note. "It took me 17 years, but I finally figured it out. I can't tell you that here because that kind of information can cause chaos." Authorities discovered salvia, a hallucinogen, in his bedroom. Chidester legally obtained the psychoactive herb online. His mother stated that he had been depressed, and she had questioned his salvia use months before his death.

Used by the Mazatec indigenous people in Mexico for spiritual purposes, salvia is known as "Diviner's Sage" and "María Pastora." The plant is part of the mint family and can be smoked or taken orally in liquid form. Characterized by intense hallucinations, the high occurs within one minute of ingestion and lasts up to five minutes, gradually fading fifteen to twenty minutes afterward. *New Scientist* writer Gaia Vince tried the drug: "My body felt disconnected from 'me' and objects and people appeared cartoonish, surreal, and marvelous. Then, as suddenly as it had begun, it was over."[2]

Chidester's death triggered a debate over salvia's safety. Some research suggests that it may produce depressive-like moods in lab animals. "We control LSD, and we should control this,"[3] argues Delaware state senator Karen Peterson. The state enacted "Brett's Law," which categorizes salvia as a Sched-

---

1. Oren Dorell, "Powerful but Legal, Hallucinogenic Under Scrutiny," *USA Today*, April 2, 2006. www.usatoday.com.
2. Gaia Vince, "Mind-Altering Drugs: Does Legal Mean Safe?" *New Scientist*, September 29, 2006.
3. Oren Dorell, "Powerful but Legal, Hallucinogenic Under Scrutiny," *USA Today*, April 2, 2006. www.usatoday.com.

ule I controlled substance. YouTube videos of users experiencing extreme reactions to salvia have also garnered national attention. As of July 2010, fourteen states have banned the drug, but it is not federally regulated.

Nonetheless, other commentators argue that no other suicides or deaths have been linked to salvia. "It's remarkable that Chidester's parents, and only Chidester's parents, continue to be cited over and over again by the mainstream media in their coverage of the supposed 'controversy' over the risks of *Salvia divinorum*,"[4] maintains Alex Coolman, a California attorney. Researcher Daniel Siebert, who has studied the drug for more than two decades, supports its responsible and therapeutic use by adults. "A sensible approach would be to regulate *Salvia divinorum* in a similar manner as alcohol and tobacco,"[5] he writes on his website. "The evidence shows that this herb is relatively safe and non-addictive."

Public awareness of salvia is increasing, animating similar discussions from the last decade about ecstasy, GHB, and other club drugs. In the following chapter, the authors offer their positions on drug use in the United States.

4. "Brett Chidester and Salvia: 'Suicide Solution" Redux," Drug Law, Policy, and Politics in California, the Ninth Circuit, and the United States, 2007.
5. Daniel Siebert, "The Legal Status of *Salvia Divinorum*," May 29, 2010. www.sage wisdom.com.

"Underlying these increases are negative shifts in teen attitudes . . . about the acceptability of drug use and drinking."

Teen Drug Abuse Has Increased

Biotech Week

Biotech Week is a newsletter published by medical news company and distributor NewsRX. In the following viewpoint, it asserts that the decade-long drop in substance abuse among American teens is reversing. According to Biotech Week, *the latest data shows that use of alcohol, marijuana, and ecstasy has significantly increased from 2008 to 2009. These troubling trends, the newsletter reports, are the results of more lax attitudes toward drugs among adolescents and the media, cuts in spending for federal prevention programs, and failure of parents to act upon suspicions that their children are experimenting or abusing drugs.*

As you read, consider the following questions:

1. What data does *Biotech Week* provide to back their assertion that more youths perceive drug abuse in more positive ways?

Biotech Week, "Partnership for a Drug-Free America; Cause for Concern: National Study Shows Reversal in Decade-long Declines in Teen Abuse of Drugs and Alcohol Anonymous," March 17, 2010. Reprinted by permission.

2. As stated in the viewpoint, how do parents help prevent drug abuse among students from seventh to twelfth grade?

3. As stated by *Biotech Week*, how does the survey characterize teen abuse of prescription drugs?

After a decade of consistent declines in teen drug abuse, a new national study released by the Partnership for a Drug-Free America and MetLife Foundation points to marked upswings in use of drugs that teens are likely to encounter at parties and in other social situations.

According to the 2009 Partnership Attitude Tracking Study [PATS], sponsored by MetLife Foundation, the number of teens in grades 9–12 that used alcohol in the past month has grown by 11 percent, (from 35 percent in 2008 to 39 percent in 2009), past year Ecstasy use shows a 67 percent increase (from 6 percent in 2008 to 10 percent in 2009) and past year marijuana use shows a 19 percent increase (from 32 percent in 2008 to 38 percent in 2009). The PATS data mark a reversal in the remarkable, sustained declines in several drugs of abuse among teens: methamphetamine (meth) was down by over 60 percent and past month alcohol and marijuana use had decreased a full 30 percent over the past decade from 1998–2008.

Negative Shifts

Underlying these increases are negative shifts in teen attitudes, particularly a growing belief in the benefits and acceptability of drug use and drinking. The percentage of teens agreeing that "being high feels good" increased significantly from 45 percent in 2008 to 51 percent in 2009, while those saying that "friends usually get high at parties" increased from 69 percent to 75 percent over the same time period. The Partnership/MetLife Foundation attitude-tracking study also found a significant drop in the number of teens agreeing strongly that they "don't want to hang around drug users"—from 35 percent in 2008 to 30 percent in 2009.

"These new PATS data should put all parents on notice that they have to pay closer attention to their kids' behavior—especially their social interactions—and they must take action just as soon as they think their child may be using drugs or drinking," said Steve Pasierb, president and CEO of the Partnership.

Dennis White, president and CEO of MetLife Foundation, added that "the earlier parents take steps to address a child's drug or alcohol use, the greater the chance they'll be effective in preventing a serious problem. We need to be sure parents know when it's time to act, and how to act when confronted with a substance abuse situation."

Time for Parents to Take Action

The resurgence in teen drug and alcohol use comes at a time when pro-drug cues in popular culture—in film, television and online—abound, and when funding for federal prevention programs has been declining for several years.

This places an even greater burden on parents. Among the parents surveyed for the PATS study, 20 percent say their child (ages 10–19) has already used drugs or alcohol beyond an "experimental" level. Among parents of teens ages 14–19, that percentage jumps to 31 percent, nearly one-third.

Disturbingly, among those parents of teens who have used, nearly half (47 percent) either waited to take action or took no action at all—which studies show put those children at greater risk of continued use and negative consequences.

"We're very troubled by this upswing that has implications not just for parents, who are the main focus of the Partnership's efforts, but for the country as a whole," said Partnership chairman Patricia Russo. "The United States simply can't afford to let millions of kids struggle through their academic and professional lives hindered by substance abuse.

Parents and caregivers need to play a more active role in protecting their families, trust their instincts and take immediate action as soon as they sense a problem."

Discovering that a teen is using drugs or drinking is often a frightening experience for parents—many feel alone, ashamed, and confused about what to do next. The Partnership encourages parents of children who are using drugs or alcohol to take action as soon as they suspect or know their child is using and provides parents with free, anonymous access to the most current, research-based information on how to help their child and their family take the next steps. Developed in collaboration with scientists from the Treatment Research Institute, Time to Act, offers step-by-step advice and sympathetic guidance from substance abuse experts, family therapists, scientists and fellow parents to help guide families through the process of understanding drug and alcohol use, confronting a child, setting boundaries and seeking outside help.

Because research tells us that kids in grades 7–12 who learn a lot about the dangers of drugs from their parents are up to 50 percent less likely to ever use, parents are encouraged to have frequent ongoing conversations with their children about the dangers of drugs and alcohol and take early action if they think their child is using or might have a problem. Parent visitors to Drugfree.org can learn to talk with their kids about drugs and alcohol and take charge of the conversation with their kids.

No Improvement in Teen Abuse of Rx and OTC Medicines, Cigarettes, Inhalants, Steroids, Heroin

According to the PATS survey, teen abuse of prescription (Rx) and over-the-counter (OTC) medicines has remained stable with about 1 in 5 teens in grades 9–12 (20 percent) or 3.2 million reporting abuse of a prescription medication at least once in their lives, and 1 in 7 teens (15 percent) or 2.4 million teens reporting abuse of a prescription pain reliever in the past year. Eight percent or 1.3 million teens have reported OTC cough medicine abuse in the past year.

PATS shows more than half or 56 percent of teens in grades 9–12 believe Rx drugs are easier to get than illegal drugs. Also, 62 percent believe most teens get Rx drugs from their own family's medicine cabinets and 63 percent believe Rx drugs are easy to get from their parent's medicine cabinet, up significantly from 56 percent just last year.

Teen smoking rates have remained stable with 25 percent of teens reporting smoking cigarettes in the past month. Teen inhalant use remains steady at 10 percent for past year use, yet only 66 percent of teens report that "sniffing or huffing things to get high can kill you," significantly less than the 70 percent of teens who agreed just last year. Inhalant abuse merits careful monitoring—as attitudes towards inhalant abuse weaken, abuse is more likely to increase. Steroid and heroin use among teens remains low at 5 percent for lifetime use.

The 21st annual national study of 3,287 teens in grades 9–12 and 804 parents is nationally projectable with a +/−2.3 percent margin of error for the teen sample and +/− 3.5 percent for the parent sample. Conducted for the Partnership and MetLife Foundation by the Roper Public Affairs division of GfK Custom Research [North America], the 2009 PATS teen study was administered in private, public and parochial schools, while the parents study was conducted through in-home interviews by de Kadt Marketing and Research, Inc. For more information or to view the full PATS report, please visit Drugfree.org.

> "The proportion of students reporting *using* any illicit drug other than mari-juana *has been gradually declining.*"

Some Teen Drug Abuse Has Decreased

Monitoring the Future

Funded by the National Institute on Drug Abuse, Monitoring the Future is a project of the University of Michigan's Institute for Social Research, which surveys youth substance abuse each year. In the following viewpoint, the project contends that rates of use for several classes of drugs declined or did not significantly change from 2008 to 2009. For instance, the use of hallucinogens and powdered cocaine dropped, Monitoring the Future states, with the use of cocaine, heroin, methamphetamine, Rohypnol, GHB, and ketamine considerably lower than their peaks. None-theless, the project warns that marijuana use is up, in part be-cause more adolescents perceive it as less risky.

As you read, consider the following questions:

1. What is Monitoring the Future's concern about the use of ecstasy despite reports that its usage has not in-creased?

Monitoring the Future, "Teen Marijuana Use Tilts Up, While Some Drugs Decline in Use," December 14, 2009. www.monitoringthefuture.org. Reprinted by permission.

2. What are the project's findings on the use of salvia?

3. What are the project's findings regarding rates of binge drinking among youths?

Marijuana use among American adolescents has been increasing gradually over the past two years (three years among 12th graders) following years of declining use, according to the latest Monitoring the Future study, which has been tracking drug use among U.S. teens since 1975.

"So far, we have not seen any dramatic rise in marijuana use, but the upward trending of the past two or three years stands in stark contrast to the steady decline that preceded it for nearly a decade," said University of Michigan researcher Lloyd Johnston, the study's principal investigator.

"Not only is use rising, but a key belief about the degree of risk associated with marijuana use has been in decline among young people even longer, and the degree to which teens disapprove of use of the drug has recently begun to decline. Changes in these beliefs and attitudes are often very influential in driving changes in use."

The proportion of young people using *any illicit drug* is also up slightly over the past two years. This measure is driven largely by marijuana use, because marijuana is the most widely used of all illicit drugs. In 2009, marijuana use in the prior 12 months (annual prevalence) was reported by about 12 percent of the nation's 8th graders, 27 percent of 10th graders, and a third of 12th graders. The proportions saying they used any illicit drug in the past year were 15 percent, 29 percent, and 37 percent.

The proportion of students reporting using *any illicit drug other than marijuana* has been gradually declining, and has continued to do so in 8th and 12th grades in 2009. The prevalence rates for using any such drug in the prior 12 months are 7 percent, 12 percent, and 17 percent in grades 8, 10, and 12.

There were declines this year in the use of several specific drug classes. High school seniors showed significant drops in their use of *LSD* and *hallucinogens other than LSD*, taken as a class, thus continuing long-term gradual declines. (Use of both of these classes of drugs had shown declines in the lower grades previously.) There was some continuing decline in all grades in the use of *cocaine*, and specifically of *powder cocaine*, with annual usage levels for cocaine reaching the lowest levels since the early 1990s.

While use of *ecstasy, inhalants*, and *LSD* is not rising currently, the investigators remain concerned because the *perceived risk* associated with those drugs has been in decline for several years and may leave young people open to renewed interest in those drugs.

The proportion of young people who see "great risk" associated with trying *ecstacy* has fallen appreciably and steadily since 2004 (2005 in the case of 12th graders).

"Given the glamorous name and reputation of this drug, I could easily imagine it making a comeback as younger children entering their teens become increasingly unaware of its risks," Johnston said. "And, while *LSD* use is at historically low levels at present, the proportion of students seeing its use as dangerous has been in decline for a long time (though it did not decline further this year in two of the three grades), removing a major obstacle to experimentation. We have seen LSD make a comeback before; clearly it could happen again."

Likewise, 8th and 10th graders, who are most likely to use *inhalants* (gases and aerosols inhaled or "huffed" in order to get high), have been showing a steady decline since 2001 in the belief that experimenting with these substances is dangerous.

"This leaves them more vulnerable to any new stimulus toward trying inhalants," Johnston noted.

While marijuana use is increasing and the use of several drugs continues to decline, the majority of illicit drugs covered in the study showed little further change this year, though most of them are at levels of use that are considerably below the recent peaks reached since the mid-1990s. These include *ecstasy, crack cocaine, heroin, narcotics other than heroin* taken as a class, *Vicodin* specifically (a narcotic analgesic), *amphetamines, methamphetamine, crystal methamphetamine, tranquilizers*, and three so-called "club drugs": *Rohypnol, GHB*, and *ketamine*.

The Prescription Drugs

Prescription drugs have received considerable attention in the past couple of years as the Monitoring the Future study documented their rising rates of use. Fortunately, none (with the possible exceptions of Adderall and OxyContin) appear to be increasing at the moment.

After several years of decline, the use of *amphetamines* outside of medical supervision did not show any significant further decrease this year; but the specific amphetamine, *Ritalin*, did show a further significant decline in annual prevalence among 12th graders. That brought their annual prevalence of Ritalin use down to only 40 percent of what it was when its use was first measured in the study in 2001. Annual use fell from 5 percent to 2 percent of 12th graders reporting any Ritalin use in the prior year that was not under a doctor's orders.

It would appear, though, that another prescription drug may be taking its place. *Adderall*, another stimulant used in the treatment of attention-deficit/hyperactivity disorder (ADHD), was included in the survey for the first time this year; in 2009 it shows annual prevalence rates of use outside of medical supervision of 2 percent, 6 percent, and 5 percent in grades 8, 10, and 12, respectively.

Sedative (barbiturate) use, which had risen considerably from 1992 through 2005, has fallen back a little since then, from an annual prevalence of 7 percent in 2004 to 5 percent in 2009 among 12th graders (8th and 10th graders do not receive this question). Similarly, *tranquilizer* use, which grew considerably in use during the 1990s and peaked in 2002 (at 8 percent annual prevalence among 12th graders), has since fallen back a bit to 6 percent in 2009. Tranquilizer use has followed a similar trajectory at 10th grade, but at 8th grade, use has not fallen back after rising. No further change was seen in 2009 for tranquilizer use at any of the three grades.

Narcotics other than heroin, taken as a class, have remained level, though at recent peak prevalence rates. Most of these drugs are opiate or opiate-type analgesics and include Vicodin and OxyContin. *Vicodin* use, while remaining at high levels, remained essentially unchanged this year (with 3 percent, 8 percent, and 10 percent of 8th-, 10th-, and 12th-grade students indicating use in the prior 12 months).

The picture for *OxyContin* is a little less clear. At all three grades, OxyContin use is higher today than it was when its use was first measured in 2002, although only 10th grade showed an increase in 2009 (+0.9 percentage points, not significant). The annual prevalence rates are now 2 percent, 5 percent, and 5 percent, respectively for OxyContin at the three grade levels. Whether this one-year increase at 10th grade is real, or simply a sampling artifact, will have to wait another year to be resolved. But the main point is that these two dangerous and highly addictive narcotic drugs remain at high levels of use among American teens.

Over-the-Counter Cough and Cold Medicines

The use of *cough and cold medicines*, like Robitussin, to get high showed no decline this year either. These over-the-counter medications usually contain the active ingredient dextromethorphan. Annual prevalence rates have not changed much since 2006, when use of these drugs was first measured. The proportions of students surveyed in 2009 who say they

Steve Pasierb, Partnership for a Drug-Free America

"Teens live in a world of social networking and connectedness—they're more open, constantly sharing their thoughts and experiences. Teens recognize the impact of use, know others with a problem and seem to attach less stigma to getting help for themselves or a friend who is in trouble."

Partnership for a Drug-Free America,
"20th Annual Teen Study Shows 25 Percent Drop in Meth Use
over Three Years; Marijuana Down 30 Percent over Ten Years,"
April 30, 2009.

have taken these drugs for the purpose of getting high in the prior 12 months are 4 percent, 6 percent, and 6 percent in grades 8, 10, and 12, respectively.

"Despite the fact that they are sold over the counter, these drugs can be dangerous when consumed in the large quantities that young people tend to use in order to get high," Johnston said.

Salvia and Provigil

Two drugs were added to the 12th-grade questionnaires this year—salvia and Provigil.

Salvia, or *salvia divinorum,* is derived from a plant grown in the mountains of Mexico. It is an herb in the mint family that can induce relatively short-acting dissociative effects when chewed, smoked, or taken as a tincture. The U.S. Drug Enforcement Administration has designated it a "drug of concern," but at present, it is not controlled under the federal Controlled Substances Act. The 2009 survey found that 6 percent of 12th graders indicated having used salvia during the prior 12 months. Clearly this drug has begun to make in-roads in the adolescent population.

The other drug added to the study in 2009 is *Provigil* (modafinil), which is a prescription-controlled medicine for improving wakefulness. It is usually prescribed to people experiencing excessive sleepiness as a result of sleep disorders due to sleep apnea, shift work, or narcolepsy. The annual prevalence of using Provigil outside of medical supervision by 12th graders in 2009 is 1.8 percent, suggesting that misuse of this drug by teens is not as yet a serious problem.

Alcohol Use

Alcohol use has generally been in a long-term, gradual decline at all three grade levels, with 30-day (or past month) prevalence having fallen from recent peak levels by over 40 percent among 8th graders, by over 25 percent among 10th graders, and by about one-sixth among 12th graders. This year only the 8th graders showed a continuation of the decline, while use in the upper grades leveled off.

Binge drinking, here defined as having five or more drinks in a row at least once in the prior two weeks, has shown similar proportional declines; again, only the 8th graders showed any indication of the decline continuing this year. (The rates in 2009 for having had any alcohol to drink in the past 30 days are 15 percent, 30 percent, and 44 percent in 8th, 10th, and 12th grade, respectively; while the two-week prevalence of binge drinking at least once in the prior two weeks are 8 percent, 18 percent, and 25 percent.)

Perceived risk for binge drinking continued to rise for 12th graders but did not in the lower grades. When asked how easy it would be to get alcohol if they wanted some, the majority of students in all three grades said it would be "fairly easy" or "very easy," but such easy availability has declined considerably in recent years in the lower grades, particularly in 8th grade.

For example, in 1996 the proportion of 8th graders saying it would be easy to get alcohol stood at its peak level of 75 percent, but by 2009 this statistic had fallen to 62 percent, including a significant decrease in 2009.

"It would appear that state and local efforts to crack down on sales to underage buyers, perhaps along with greater parental vigilance, have had an effect," Johnston said.

Steroids

Teenage use of anabolic steroids increased in the late 1990s, reaching peak levels in 2000 among 8th graders, in 2002 among 10th graders, and 2004 among 12th graders. Since those recent peaks, however, annual prevalence of steroid use has declined considerably—by about half in grade 8, by nearly two-thirds in grade 10, and by 40 percent in grade 12. In 2009, the proportions reporting any use of anabolic steroids in the past year were only 0.8 percent, 0.8 percent, and 1.5 percent in grades 8, 10, and 12, respectively. Among boys, who have considerably higher use than girls, the rates were 1.0 percent, 1.2 percent, and 2.5 percent.

> "Millions of Americans have health problems caused by smoking."

Smoking Causes Significant Health Problems

National Cancer Institute

In the following viewpoint, the National Cancer Institute (NCI) claims that tobacco smoke—which contains 250 known dangerous chemicals—harms a person's overall health and affects almost every organ in the human body. It is the leading cause of cancer, the institute warns, and is associated with heart disease and stroke as well as chronic bronchitis, emphysema, and other airway infections. Moreover, NCI asserts that pregnant smokers risk premature births and abnormally low weights for their unborn babies. The benefits of quitting, the institute offers, are both immediate and long term, from improved circulation within a few weeks to significantly reducing premature death. NCI is part of the US National Institutes of Health.

As you read, consider the following questions:

1. What types of cancers does smoking cause, according to NCI?

National Cancer Institute, "Quitting Smoking: Why to Quit and How to Get Help," Aug 17, 2007. www.cancer.gov. Reprinted by permission.

2. As stated by the institute, what are some of the harmful chemicals found in tobacco smoke?

3. The risk of premature death and developing cancer depends on what factors, as described by NCI?

Smoking harms nearly every organ of the body and diminishes a person's overall health. Smoking is a leading cause of cancer and of death from cancer. It causes cancers of the lungs, esophagus, larynx (voice box), mouth, throat, kidneys, bladder, pancreas, stomach, and cervix as well as acute myeloid leukemia.

Smoking also causes heart disease, stroke, lung disease (chronic bronchitis and emphysema), hip fractures, and cataracts. Smokers are at higher risk of developing pneumonia and other airway infections.

A pregnant smoker is at higher risk of having her baby born too early and with an abnormally low weight. A woman who smokes during or after pregnancy increases her infant's risk of death from sudden infant death syndrome (SIDS).

Millions of Americans have health problems caused by smoking. Cigarette smoking and exposure to tobacco smoke cause an estimated average of 438,000 premature deaths each year in the United States. Of these premature deaths, about 40 percent are from cancer, 35 percent are from heart disease and stroke, and 25 percent are from lung disease. Smoking is the leading cause of premature, preventable death in this country.

Regardless of their age, smokers can substantially reduce their risk of disease, including cancer, by quitting.

Does Tobacco Smoke Contain Harmful Chemicals?

Yes. Tobacco smoke contains chemicals that are harmful to both smokers and nonsmokers. Breathing even a little tobacco smoke can be harmful. Of the 4,000 chemicals in tobacco smoke, at least 250 are known to be harmful. The toxic chemicals found in smoke include hydrogen cyanide (used in chemical weapons), carbon monoxide (found in car exhaust), formaldehyde (used as an embalming fluid), ammonia (used in household cleaners), and toluene (found in paint thinners).

Of the 250 known harmful chemicals in tobacco smoke, more than 50 have been found to cause cancer. These chemicals include:

- arsenic (a heavy metal toxin)

- benzene (a chemical found in gasoline)

- beryllium (a toxic metal)

- cadmium (a metal used in batteries)

- chromium (a metallic element)

- ethylene oxide (a chemical used to sterilize medical devices)

- nickel (a metallic element)

- polonium–210 (a chemical element that gives off radiation)

- vinyl chloride (a toxic substance used in plastics manufacture)

What Are the Immediate Benefits of Quitting Smoking?

The immediate health benefits of quitting smoking are substantial. Heart rate and blood pressure, which were abnormally high while smoking, begin to return to normal. Within a few hours, the level of carbon monoxide in the blood begins to decline. (Carbon monoxide, a colorless, odorless gas found in cigarette smoke, reduces the blood's ability to carry oxygen.) Within a few weeks, people who quit smoking have improved circulation, don't produce as much phlegm, and don't cough or wheeze as often. Within several months of quitting, people can expect significant improvements in lung function.

No Safe Smoke

Some people try to make their smoking habit safer by smoking fewer cigarettes, but most smokers find that hard to do. Research has found that even smoking as few as 1 to 4 cigarettes a day can lead to serious health outcomes, including an increased risk of heart disease and a greater chance of dying at a younger age.

Some people think that switching from high-tar and high-nicotine cigarettes to those with low tar and nicotine makes smoking safer, but this is not true. When people switch to brands with lower tar and nicotine, they often end up smoking more cigarettes, or more of each cigarette, to get the same nicotine dose as before.

Smokers have been led to believe that "light" cigarettes are a lower health risk and are a good option to quitting. This is not true. A low-tar cigarette can be just as harmful as a high-tar cigarette because a person often takes deeper puffs, puffs more often, or smokes them to a shorter butt length. Studies have not found that the risk of lung cancer is any lower in smokers of "light" or low-tar cigarettes.

American Cancer Society,
"Questions About Smoking, Tobacco, and Health,"
Cancer.org, 2009.

What Are the Long-Term Benefits of Quitting Smoking?

Quitting smoking reduces the risk of cancer and other diseases, such as heart disease and lung disease, caused by smoking. People who quit smoking, regardless of their age, are less likely than those who continue to smoke to die from smoking-related illness. Studies have shown that quitting at about age 30 reduces the chance of dying from smoking-related diseases by more than 90 percent. People who quit at about age 50 reduce their risk of dying prematurely by 50 percent compared with those who continue to smoke. Even people who quit at about age 60 or older live longer than those who continue to smoke.

Does Quitting Smoking Lower the Risk of Cancer?

Quitting smoking substantially reduces the risk of developing and dying from cancer, and this benefit increases the longer a person remains smoke free. However, even after many years of not smoking, the risk of lung cancer in former smokers remains higher than in people who have never smoked.

The risk of premature death and the chance of developing cancer due to cigarettes depend on the number of years of smoking, the number of cigarettes smoked per day, the age at which smoking began, and the presence or absence of illness at the time of quitting. For people who have already developed cancer, quitting smoking reduces the risk of developing a second cancer.

Should Someone Already Diagnosed with Cancer Bother to Quit Smoking?

Yes. There are many reasons that people diagnosed with cancer should quit smoking. For those having surgery or other treatments, quitting smoking helps improve the body's ability to heal and respond to the cancer treatment, and it lowers the risk of pneumonia and respiratory failure. Also, quitting smoking may lower the risk of the cancer returning or a second cancer forming.

What Are Some of the Challenges Associated with Quitting Smoking?

Quitting smoking may cause short-term problems, especially for those who have smoked a large number of cigarettes for a long period of time:

- Feeling sad or anxious: People who quit smoking are likely to feel depressed, anxious, irritable, and restless, and may have difficulty sleeping or concentrating.

- Gaining weight: Increased appetite is a common withdrawal symptom after quitting smoking, and studies show that people who quit smoking increase their food intake. Although most smokers gain less than 10 pounds, for some people the weight gain can be troublesome. Regular physical activity can help people maintain a healthy weight.

Depression, anxiety, restlessness, weight gain, and other problems are symptoms of nicotine withdrawal. Many people find that nicotine replacement products and other medicines may relieve these problems. However, even without medication, withdrawal symptoms and other problems do subside over time. It helps to keep in mind that people who kick the smoking habit have the opportunity for a healthier future.

Can a Doctor, Dentist, or Pharmacist Help a Person Quit Smoking?

Doctors, dentists, and pharmacists can be good sources of information about the health risks of smoking and the benefits of quitting. They can describe the proper use and potential side effects of nicotine replacement therapy and other medicines, and they can help people find local quit smoking resources.

How Can I Help Someone I Know Quit Smoking?

It's understandable to be concerned about someone you know who currently smokes. It's important to find out if this person wants to quit smoking. Most smokers say they want to quit. If they don't want to quit, try to find out why.

Here are some things you can do to help:

- Express things in terms of your own concern about the smoker's health ("I'm worried about . . .").

- Acknowledge that the smoker may get something out of smoking and may find it difficult to quit.

- Be encouraging and express your faith that the smoker can quit for good.

- Suggest a specific action, such as calling a smoking quit line, for help in quitting smoking.

- Ask the smoker for ways you can provide support.

Here are two things you should not do:

- Don't send quit smoking materials to smokers unless they ask for them.

- Don't criticize, nag, or remind the smoker about past failures.

What Are Nicotine Replacement Products?

Nicotine is the substance in cigarettes and other forms of tobacco that causes addiction. Nicotine replacement products deliver small, measured doses of nicotine into the body, which helps to relieve the cravings and withdrawal symptoms often felt by people trying to quit smoking. Strong and consistent evidence shows that nicotine replacement products can help people quit smoking.

It's far less harmful for a person to get nicotine from a nicotine replacement product than from cigarettes because tobacco smoke contains many toxic and cancer-causing substances. Long-term use of nicotine replacement products is not known to be associated with any serious harmful effects.

| "*There are many reasons to be skeptical about what professional anti-smoking advocates say.*"

Smoking-Related Health Problems Are Exaggerated

Maureen Martin and Joseph L. Bast

In the following viewpoint, Maureen Martin and Joseph L. Bast contend that dominant perceptions of smoking and health are skewed. Cigarettes are unhealthy, but the authors allege that the supposed mortality rates of smoking and dangers of secondhand smoke are based on faulty science. Also, Martin and Bast maintain that the health effects and risks can be, in fact, reduced greatly by switching to filtered, low-tar cigarettes and smokeless tobacco. Nonetheless, major antismoking foundations and abusive lawyers continue to demonize cigarettes and tobacco, the authors assert. Martin is a senior fellow at the Heartland Institute, a Chicago-based, libertarian think tank, of which Bast is president.

As you read, consider the following questions:

1. What data do Martin and Bast cite to support their conclusion that the odds of a lifelong smoker dying prematurely are only twelve to one?

Maureen Martin and Joseph L. Bast, "Overview: Tobacco and Freedom," Heartland.org, 2006. Reprinted by permission.

2. What do James Enstrom and Geoffrey Kabat state about secondhand smoke and the risk of lung cancer?

3. What is the authors' position on government regulation of smoking?

Everywhere you look, anti-smoking groups are campaigning against smokers. They claim smoking kills one-third or even half of all smokers; that secondhand smoke is a major public health problem; that smokers impose enormous costs on the rest of society; and that for all these reasons, taxes on cigarettes should be raised.

There are many reasons to be skeptical about what professional anti-smoking advocates say. They personally profit by exaggerating the health threats of smoking and winning passage of higher taxes and bans on smoking in public places. The anti-smoking movement is hardly a grassroots phenomenon: It is largely funded by taxpayers and a few major foundations with left-liberal agendas.

A growing number of independent policy experts from a wide range of professions and differing political views are speaking out against the anti-smoking campaign. They defend smokers for several reasons:

- Smokers already pay taxes that are too high to be fair, and far above any cost they impose on the rest of society.

- The public health community's campaign to demonize smokers and all forms of tobacco is based on junk science.

- Litigation against the tobacco industry is an example of lawsuit abuse, and has "loaded the gun" for lawsuits against other industries.

- Smoking bans hurt small businesses and violate private property rights.

- The harm caused by smoking can be reduced by educating smokers about their options.

- Punishing smokers "for their own good" is repulsive to the basic libertarian principles that ought to limit the use of government force.

Taxing Smokers

Cigarettes are already the most heavily taxed commodity in the U.S. The federal excise tax is $0.39 a pack and the national average state excise tax is about $0.60 per pack, for a total of $0.99 per pack. In addition, the 1998 [Tobacco] Master Settlement Agreement (MSA) increased the price of a pack of cigarettes by about $0.40 a pack. In a growing number of cities, a pack-a-day smoker pays more in cigarette taxes than he or she pays in state income taxes.

Such high and discriminatory taxes on smokers are unfair. They are also an inefficient and unreliable way to raise funds for government. Excise taxes require regular rate increases to keep pace with inflation, whereas income, sales, and property taxes all rise with inflation or economic growth. Because of their narrow bases, excise taxes are unstable revenue generators. And excise taxes require relatively high rates to raise funds. These rates, in turn, create opportunities for evasion and the transfer of economic activity to states with lower taxes.

Dramatic price hikes and extreme taxes on cigarettes are threatening to create a stampede of tax evasion, black market transactions, counterfeiting, and even use of lethal violence against convenience store clerks and truck drivers. Tax hikes of $1.00 a pack or more, as have been adopted recently by New York; Cook County, Illinois; and elsewhere threaten to take us to a neo-prohibitionist era, with all the crime, expenses, and loss of respect for law enforcement that accompanied Prohibition.

Excise taxes are also regressive. People with low incomes not only pay a higher percentage of their incomes on cigarette taxes than do wealthier people, they even pay more in absolute terms. Persons earning less than $10,000 paid an average of $81 a year in tobacco taxes, versus $49 for those who make $50,000 or more. This was before recent massive tax hikes!

Social Costs

Are high taxes on cigarettes justified by the social costs smokers impose on the rest of society? No.

Harvard professor Kip Viscusi has repeatedly demonstrated that smokers already pay more in excise taxes than the social costs of their habits. Even before the MSA, "excise taxes on cigarettes equal or exceed the medical care costs associated with smoking." For example, Illinois's cigarette taxes, according to Viscusi, were $0.13 more per pack than the social costs of smoking before the settlement added $0.40 to the price of a pack of cigarettes, before the $0.40 a pack tax hike approved by the state legislature in 2002, and before Cook County's $0.82 a pack boost in 2004.

Instead of raising cigarette taxes, simple justice demands that cigarette taxes be reduced to zero. In fact, states should consider taping a dime or a quarter to every pack of cigarettes as a way of thanking smokers for reducing the burden on taxpayers!

Junk Science

How harmful is smoking to smokers? Public health advocates who claim one out of every three, or even one out of every two, smokers will die from a smoking-related illness are grossly exaggerating the real threat. The actual odds of a smoker dying from smoking before the age of 75 are about 1 in 12. In other words, 11 out of 12 lifelong smokers don't die before the age of 75 from a smoking-related disease.

In a 1998 article titled "Lies, Damned Lies, and 400,000 Smoking-Related Deaths," [Robert A.] Levy and [Rosalind]

Marimont showed how removing diseases for which a link between smoking and mortality has been alleged but not proven cuts the hypothetical number of smoking-related fatalities in half. Replacing an unrealistically low death rate for never-smokers with the real fatality rate cuts the number by a third.

Controlling for "confounding factors"—such as the fact that smokers tend to exercise less, drink more, and accept high-risk jobs—reduces the estimated number of deaths by about half again. Instead of 400,000 smoking-related deaths a year, Levy and Marimont estimate the number to be around 100,000.

This would place the lifetime odds of dying from smoking at 6 to 1 (45 million smokers divided by 100,000 deaths per year x 75 years), rather than 3 to 1. However, about half (45 percent) of all smoking-related deaths occur at age 75 or higher. Calling these deaths "premature" is stretching common usage of the word. The odds of a lifelong smoker dying prematurely of a smoking-related disease, then, are about 12 to 1.

Secondhand Smoke

Is secondhand smoke a rationale for higher taxes on tobacco or smoking bans? The research used to justify government regulation of secondhand smoke has been powerfully challenged by critics, including Congress's own research bureau. According to the EPA [Environmental Protection Agency], the risk ratio for forty years of exposure to a pack-a-day smoker is just 1.19. Epidemiologists as a rule are skeptical of any relative risks lower than 3 and dismiss as random ratios less than 1.3. Science writer Michael Fumento and others have documented how the threat of secondhand smoke has been greatly exaggerated.

The latest word on second[hand] smoke appeared in the May 12, 2003, issue of the *British Medical Journal*. Two epidemiologists, James Enstrom at UCLA [University of California, Los Angeles] and Geoffrey Kabat at the State University of

New York at Stony Brook, analyzed data collected by the American Cancer Society from more than 100,000 Californians from 1959 through 1997.

"The results do not support a causal relation between environmental tobacco smoke and tobacco-related mortality," the researchers wrote, although they do not rule out a small effect. "The association between tobacco smoke and coronary heart disease and lung cancer may be considerably weaker than generally believed."

"It is generally considered that exposure to environmental tobacco smoke is roughly equivalent to smoking one cigarette per day," according to Enstrom and Kabat. "If so, a small increase in lung cancer is possible, but the commonly reported 30 percent increase in heart disease risk—the purported cause of almost all the deaths attributed to secondhand smoke—is highly implausible."

Smoking Bans

Concern over the health effects of smoking and secondhand smoke has led to calls for bans on smoking in public spaces. Are these bans justified?

Most seats in most restaurants are already designated nonsmoking, and there is little evidence that nonsmokers who visit restaurants and bars believe smoking is a major concern. In restaurants with smoking and nonsmoking sections, better ventilation systems rather than smoking bans can solve any remaining concerns.

Smoking bans have had severe negative effects on restaurants, bars, and nightclubs in cities where such bans have been enacted. Smokers choose to stay home or visit with friends who allow smoking in their homes, or spend less time (and less money) in bars and nightclubs before leaving. Smoking bans can also move noisy and potentially dangerous crowds onto sidewalks, and divert police resources from battling more serious crime.

Lawsuit Abuse

"The states' legal crusade against the tobacco industry will one day rank as one of the worst developments in American public law in the twentieth century," wrote Michael DeBow, a professor of law at Cumberland School of Law, Samford University.

In 1998, Philip Morris and other major tobacco companies settled a lawsuit brought by 46 states and five territories, promising them an astounding $243 billion over 25 years, and then approximately $18 billion a year in perpetuity. The cost of this so-called [Tobacco] Master Settlement Agreement (MSA) is entirely passed through to smokers; it is not paid by "tobacco companies." The agreement has already dramatically increased the retail price of cigarettes.

The MSA was supposed to end litigation against tobacco companies, but lawsuits continue to be filed anyway, with irresponsible juries awarding millions and even billions of dollars to smokers who knew the risks but continued to smoke anyway. Besides thousands of frivolous civil suits pursued by lawyers who long ago forgot the meaning of justice, the U.S. Justice Department is still pursuing a legal case against the tobacco industry initiated by the [Bill] Clinton administration.

The MSA also "loaded the gun" for trial lawyers to go after other industries, generating approximately $13.75 billion in projected payments to lawyers. It was, wrote DeBow, "the largest transfer of wealth as a result of litigation in the history of the human race, a transfer that is being and will continue to be financed almost entirely by smokers paying higher prices for cigarettes."

Smokers' Rights

Another reason to oppose the current campaign against smokers is because it violates the legitimate rights of smokers. John Stuart Mill, in a slender book published in 1859 titled *On Liberty*, wrote: "The only purpose for which power can be rightfully exercised over any member of a civilized community against his will is to prevent harm to others. His own good, either physical or moral, is not a sufficient warrant." This is the basic premise of libertarianism, the political philosophy of the Founding Fathers.

Mill's statement is directly applicable to the controversy over smoking. Quite simply, a just government does not have the authority to ban smoking on private property or to tell smokers to quit or to punish them if they do not. Smokers are adults, not children, and they deserve to have their informed choices respected by others.

If we pass laws forcing smokers to change their behavior "for their own good," we need to ask: Where do we stop? Do we pass laws against smoking in private homes? Against frying food indoors (which also releases known carcinogens into the air)? Eating the wrong kinds of food? Eating too much? Weighing too much? Drinking too much (and not just when driving)? Exercising too little? Should we ban other risky be-havior, such as skydiving, bungee-jumping, or riding motor-cycles? How about drinking more than one cup of coffee each day?

Harm Reduction

Anti-smoking activists give smokers a stark choice: Stop smok-ing or die! In fact, there is a third path: reduce the harm by shifting to less hazardous kinds of tobacco products. For ex-ample, moving from unfiltered to filtered cigarettes, and from regular to "low tar" cigarettes, both appear to reduce the risk of lung cancer. Switching from cigarettes to chewing tobacco dramatically reduces the health risk.

For many years, Swedes have used a kind of "spitless to-bacco" called "snus." At least partly because of the widespread use of snus, Switzerland has the lowest rate of cigarette smok-ing and lung cancer in Europe. Surely there are lessons here for U.S. tobacco policy.

Unfortunately, in the U.S., advertising the comparative health effects of different tobacco products is strongly discour-aged by the FDA [Food and Drug Administration], state attor-neys general, the courts, and a variety of government-funded, anti-tobacco organizations. As a result, few smokers know that the health risks of smoking can be dramatically reduced sim-ply by reducing the number of cigarettes smoked or by switch-ing to filtered and light cigarettes or to chewing tobacco.

Underage Smoking

Kids shouldn't smoke cigarettes, but what is the best way to discourage underage smoking? The tobacco industry is work-ing hard to enforce minimum age standards by pushing retail-ers to require proof of age at the time of purchase. Despite hysteria from the anti-smoking establishment on this matter, cigarette advertising does not target young people.

Saying we need high taxes on cigarettes to discourage teenagers from smoking is dishonest, since most teenage smokers don't buy their cigarettes, and get them instead from parents and adult friends. It is unfair to impose dramatically higher taxes on the adults who buy 95 percent or more of all cigarettes sold in order to make cigarettes less attractive to the few teenagers who actually pay for their cigarettes.

"The risks for addiction to prescription drugs increase when the drugs are used in ways other than for those prescribed."

Prescription Drug Abuse Is a Serious Problem

National Institute on Drug Abuse

The nonmedical use of and addictions to medications affect many Americans, the National Institute on Drug Abuse (NIDA) claims in the following viewpoint. NIDA states that the categories of the most abused prescriptions are opioids (used to alleviate pain), central nervous system depressants (used for sleep and anxiety disorders), and stimulants (used to treat hyperactivity and narcolepsy). Trends of such drug abuse among older adults and adolescents are areas of concern, the institute adds, with each group facing unique dangers and risk factors. NIDA is a branch of the National Institutes of Health.

As you read, consider the following questions:

1. What are the possible consequences of opioid abuse, as described by NIDA?

National Institute on Drug Abuse, "Prescription Drugs: Abuse and Addiction," *Research Report Series*, July 2001, revised 2005. Reprinted by permission.

2. In the institute's view, what are the gender differences in prescription abuse?

3. What ways can pharmacists help prevent the misuse of medications, according to NIDA?

Although most people take prescription medications responsibly, there has been an increase in the nonmedical use of or, as NIDA [National Institute on Drug Abuse] refers to it in this [viewpoint], abuse of prescription drugs in the United States.

What are some of the commonly abused prescription drugs?

Although many prescription drugs can be abused, there are several classifications of medications that are commonly abused.

The three classes of prescription drugs that are most commonly abused are:

- Opioids, which are most often prescribed to treat pain;

- Central nervous system (CNS) depressants, which are used to treat anxiety and sleep disorders; and

- Stimulants, which are prescribed to treat the sleep disorder narcolepsy and attention-deficit/hyperactivity disorder (ADHD).

Opioids

What are opioids?

Opioids are commonly prescribed because of their effective analgesic, or pain-relieving, properties. Medications that fall within this class—referred to as prescription narcotics—include morphine (e.g., Kadian, Avinza), codeine, oxycodone (e.g., OxyContin, Percodan, Percocet), and related drugs. Morphine, for example, is often used before and after surgical procedures to alleviate severe pain. Codeine, on the other hand, is often prescribed for mild pain. In addition to their pain-relieving properties, some of these drugs—codeine and diphe-noxylate (Lomotil) for example—can be used to relieve coughs and diarrhea.

How do opioids affect the brain and body?

Opioids act on the brain and body by attaching to specific proteins called opioid receptors, which are found in the brain, spinal cord, and gastrointestinal tract. When these drugs attach to certain opioid receptors, they can block the perception of pain. Opioids can produce drowsiness, nausea, constipation, and, depending upon the amount of drug taken, depress respiration. Opioid drugs also can induce euphoria by affecting the brain regions that mediate what we perceive as pleasure. This feeling is often intensified for those who abuse opioids when administered by routes other than those recommended. For example, OxyContin often is snorted or injected to enhance its euphoric effects, while at the same time increasing the risk for serious medical consequences, such as opioid overdose.

What are the possible consequences of opioid use and abuse?

Taken as directed, opioids can be used to manage pain effectively. Many studies have shown that the properly managed, short-term medical use of opioid analgesic drugs is safe and rarely causes addiction—defined as the compulsive and uncontrollable use of drugs despite adverse consequences—or dependence, which occurs when the body adapts to the presence of a drug, and often results in withdrawal symptoms when that drug is reduced or stopped. Withdrawal symptoms include restlessness, muscle and bone pain, insomnia, diarrhea, vomiting, cold flashes with goose bumps ("cold turkey"), and involuntary leg movements. Long-term use of opioids can lead to physical dependence and addiction. Taking a large single dose of an opioid could cause severe respiratory depression that can lead to death.

Is it safe to use opioid drugs with other medications?

Only under a physician's supervision can opioids be used safely with other drugs. Typically, they should not be used with other substances that depress the CNS [central nervous system], such as alcohol, antihistamines, barbiturates, benzodiazepines, or general anesthetics, because these combinations increase the risk of life-threatening respiratory depression.

CNS Depressants

What are CNS depressants?

CNS depressants, sometimes referred to as sedatives and tranquilizers, are substances that can slow normal brain function. Because of this property, some CNS depressants are useful in the treatment of anxiety and sleep disorders. Among the medications that are commonly prescribed for these purposes are the following:

- Barbiturates, such as mephobarbital (Mebaral) and pentobarbital sodium (Nembutal), are used to treat anxiety, tension, and sleep disorders.

- Benzodiazepines, such as diazepam (Valium), chlordiazepoxide HCl (Librium), and alprazolam (Xanax), are prescribed to treat anxiety, acute stress reactions, and panic attacks. The more sedating benzodiazepines, such as triazolam (Halcion) and estazolam (ProSom), are prescribed for short-term treatment of sleep disorders. Usually, benzodiazepines are not prescribed for long-term use.

How do CNS depressants affect the brain and body?

There are numerous CNS depressants; most act on the brain by affecting the neurotransmitter gamma-aminobutyric acid (GABA). Neurotransmitters are brain chemicals that facilitate communication between brain cells. GABA works by decreasing brain activity. Although the different classes of CNS depressants work in unique ways, it is through their ability to increase GABA activity that they produce a drowsy or calming effect that is beneficial to those suffering from anxiety or sleep disorders.

What are the possible consequences of CNS depressant use and abuse?

Despite their many beneficial effects, barbiturates and benzodiazepines have the potential for abuse and should be used only as prescribed. During the first few days of taking a prescribed CNS depressant, a person usually feels sleepy and uncoordinated, but as the body becomes accustomed to the effects of the drug, these feelings begin to disappear. If one uses these drugs long term, the body will develop tolerance for the drugs, and larger doses will be needed to achieve the same initial effects. Continued use can lead to physical dependence and—when use is reduced or stopped—withdrawal. Because all CNS depressants work by slowing the brain's activity, when an individual stops taking them, the brain's activity can rebound and race out of control, potentially leading to seizures and other harmful consequences. Although withdrawal from benzodiazepines can be problematic, it is rarely life threatening, whereas withdrawal from prolonged use of other CNS depressants can have life-threatening complications. Therefore, someone who is thinking about discontinuing CNS depressant therapy or who is suffering withdrawal from a CNS depressant should speak with a physician or seek medical treatment.

Is it safe to use CNS depressants with other medications?

CNS depressants should be used in combination with other medications only under a physician's close supervision. Typically, they should not be combined with any other medication or substance that causes CNS depression, including prescription pain medicines, some OTC [over-the-counter] cold and allergy medications, and alcohol. Using CNS depressants with these other substances—particularly alcohol—can slow both the heart and respiration and may lead to death.

Stimulants

What are stimulants?

As the name suggests, stimulants increase alertness, attention, and energy, as well as elevate blood pressure and increase heart rate and respiration. Stimulants historically were used to treat asthma and other respiratory problems, obesity, neurological disorders, and a variety of other ailments. But as their potential for abuse and addiction became apparent, the medical use of stimulants began to wane. Now, stimulants are prescribed for the treatment of only a few health conditions, including narcolepsy, ADHD [attention-deficit/hyperactivity disorder], and depression that has not responded to other treatments.

How do stimulants affect the brain and body?

Stimulants, such as dextroamphetamine (Dexedrine and Adderall) and methylphenidate (Ritalin and Concerta), have chemical structures similar to a family of key brain neurotransmitters called monoamines, which include norepinephrine and dopamine. Stimulants enhance the effects of these chemicals in the brain. Stimulants also increase blood pressure and heart rate, constrict blood vessels, increase blood glucose, and open up the pathways of the respiratory system. The increase in dopamine is associated with a sense of euphoria that can accompany the use of these drugs.

What are the possible consequences of stimulant use and abuse?

As with other drugs of abuse, it is possible for individuals to become dependent upon or addicted to many stimulants. Withdrawal symptoms associated with discontinuing stimulant use include fatigue, depression, and disturbance of sleep patterns. Repeated use of some stimulants over a short period can lead to feelings of hostility or paranoia. Further, taking high doses of a stimulant may result in dangerously high body temperature and an irregular heartbeat. There is also the potential for cardiovascular failure or lethal seizures.

Dangerous and Incorrect

Many teens believe that prescription drugs are less harmful than illegal drugs. Because these drugs are prescribed by doctors, teens think the substances must be safe. That, doctors warn, is a dangerous and incorrect assumption. Prescription medicines are potent, have side effects, and may be addictive, which is why they are meant to be taken under a doctor's supervision.

Current Events, a Weekly Reader Publication, *"Prescription for Danger: A Recent Report Shows Troubling Trends in Teen Abuse," March 5, 2007.*

Is it safe to use stimulants with other medications?

Stimulants should be used in combination with other medications only under a physician's supervision. Patients also should be aware of the dangers associated with mixing stimulants and OTC cold medicines that contain decongestants; combining these substances may cause blood pressure to become dangerously high or lead to irregular heart rhythms.

Trends in Prescription Drug Abuse

Although prescription drug abuse affects many Americans, some concerning trends can be seen among older adults, adolescents, and women. Several indicators suggest that prescription drug abuse is on the rise in the United States. According to the 2003 National Survey on Drug Use and Health (NSDUH), an estimated 4.7 million Americans used prescription drugs nonmedically for the first time in 2002—

- 2.5 million used pain relievers

- 1.2 million used tranquilizers

- 761,000 used stimulants

- 225,000 used sedatives

Pain reliever incidence increased—from 573,000 initiates in 1990 to 2.5 million initiates in 2000—and has remained stable through 2003. In 2002, more than half (55 percent) of the new users were females, and more than half (56 percent) were ages 18 or older.

The Drug Abuse Warning Network (DAWN), which monitors medications and illicit drugs reported in emergency departments (EDs) across the nation, recently found that two of the most frequently reported prescription medications in drug abuse-related cases are benzodiazepines (e.g., diazepam, alprazolam, clonazepam and lorazepam) and opioid pain relievers (e.g., oxycodone, hydrocodone, morphine, methadone, and combinations that include these drugs). In 2002, benzodiazepines accounted for 100,784 mentions that were classified as drug abuse cases, and opioid pain relievers accounted for more than 119,000 ED mentions. From 1994 to 2002, ED mentions of hydrocodone and oxycodone increased by 170 percent and 450 percent, respectively. While ED visits attributed to drug addiction and drug taking for psychoactive effects have been increasing, intentional overdose visits have remained stable since 1995.

Older Adults. Persons 65 years of age and above comprise only 13 percent of the population, yet account for approximately one-third of all medications prescribed in the United States. Older patients are more likely to be prescribed long-term and multiple prescriptions, which could lead to unintentional misuse.

The elderly also are at risk for prescription drug abuse, in which they intentionally take medications that are not medically necessary. In addition to prescription medications, a large percentage of older adults also use OTC medicines and dietary supplements. Because of their high rates of comorbid illnesses, changes in drug metabolism with age, and the potential for drug interactions, prescription and OTC drug abuse and misuse can have more adverse health consequences among the elderly than are likely to be seen in a younger population. Elderly persons who take benzodiazepines are at increased risk for cognitive impairment associated with benzodiazepine use, leading to possible falls (causing hip and thigh fractures), as well as vehicle accidents. However, cognitive impairment may be reversible once the drug is discontinued.

Adolescents and Young Adults. Data from the 2003 NSDUH indicate that 4.0 percent of youth ages 12 to 17 reported non-medical use of prescription medications in the past month. Rates of abuse were highest among the 18–25 age group (6.0 percent). Among the youngest group surveyed, ages 12–13, a higher percentage reported using psychotherapeutics (1.8 percent) than marijuana (1.0 percent).

The NIDA Monitoring the Future survey of 8th, 10th, and 12th graders found that the nonmedical use of opioids, tranquilizers, sedatives/barbiturates, and amphetamines was unchanged between 2003 and 2004. Specifically, the survey found that 5.0 percent of 12th graders reported using OxyContin without a prescription in the past year, and 9.3 percent reported using Vicodin, making Vicodin one of the most commonly abused licit drugs in this population. Past-year, nonmedical use of tranquilizers (e.g., Valium, Xanax) in 2004 was 2.5 percent for 8th graders, 5.1 percent for 10th graders, and 7.3 percent for 12th graders. Also within the past year, 6.5 percent of 12th graders used sedatives/barbiturates (e.g., Amytal, Nembutal) nonmedically, and 10.0 percent used amphetamines (e.g., Ritalin, Benzedrine).

Youth who use other drugs are more likely to abuse prescription medications. According to the 2001 National Household Survey on Drug Abuse (now the NSDUH), 63 percent of youth who had used prescription drugs nonmedically in the past year had also used marijuana in the past year, compared with 17 percent of youth who had not used prescription drugs nonmedically in the past year.

Gender Differences. Studies suggest that women are more likely than men to be prescribed an abusable prescription drug, particularly narcotics and antianxiety drugs—in some cases, 55 percent more likely.

Overall, men and women have roughly similar rates of nonmedical use of prescription drugs. An exception is found among 12- to 17-year-olds. In this age group, young women are more likely than young men to use psychotherapeutic drugs nonmedically. In addition, research has shown that women are at increased risk for nonmedical use of narcotic analgesics and tranquilizers (e.g., benzodiazepines).

Preventing and Recognizing Prescription Drug Abuse. The risks for addiction to prescription drugs increase when the drugs are used in ways other than for those prescribed. Health care providers, primary care physicians, and pharmacists, as well as patients themselves, all can play a role in identifying and preventing prescription drug abuse.

Physicians. Because about 70 percent of Americans (approximately 191 million people) visit their primary care physician at least once every 2 years, these doctors are in a unique position—not only to prescribe medications, but also to identify prescription drug abuse when it exists, help the patient recognize the problem, set recovery goals, and seek appropriate treatment. Screening for prescription drug abuse can be incorporated into routine medical visits by asking about substance abuse history, current prescription and OTC use, and reasons for use. Doctors should take note of rapid increases in the amount of medication needed, or frequent, unscheduled refill requests. Doctors also should be alert to the fact that those addicted to prescription drugs may engage in "doctor shopping"—moving from provider to provider—in an effort to obtain multiple prescriptions for the drug(s) they abuse.

Preventing or stopping prescription drug abuse is an important part of patient care. However, health care providers should not avoid prescribing or administering stimulants, CNS depressants, or opioid pain relievers if needed.

Pharmacists. By providing clear information on how to take a medication appropriately and describing possible side effects or drug interactions, pharmacists also can play a key role in preventing prescription drug abuse. Moreover, by monitoring prescriptions for falsification or alterations and being aware of potential "doctor shopping," pharmacists can be the first line of defense in recognizing prescription drug abuse. Some pharmacies have developed hotlines to alert other pharmacies in the region when a fraudulent prescription is detected.

Patients. There are also steps a patient can take to ensure that they use prescription medications appropriately. Patients should always follow the prescribed directions, be aware of potential interactions with other drugs, never stop or change a dosing regimen without first discussing it with their health care provider, and never use another person's prescription. Patients should inform their health care professionals about all the prescription and OTC medicines and dietary and herbal supplements they are taking, in addition to a full description of their presenting complaint, before they obtain any other medications.

| *"But as usual with drugs coverage, the press doesn't recognize its own responsibility in the devil's creation."*

The Media Have Exaggerated the Prescription Drug Abuse Crisis

Maia Szalavitz

In the following viewpoint, Maia Szalavitz alleges that the media overstate the death and addiction rates due to the use of prescription drugs, which is counterproductive. Because of the demonization of OxyContin—a prescription painkiller—in the news, she suggests that physicians became reluctant to prescribe it, choosing methadone in its place. However, the author maintains that methadone is a more dangerous drug, and while hyping its dangers, the media do not accurately inform the public about medications. Szalavitz is a journalist and co-author of Recovery Options: The Complete Guide: How You and Your Loved Ones Can Understand and Treat Alcohol and Other Drug Problems.

Maia Szalavitz, "Welcome to the New Drug Scare of 2007," STATS.org, September 27, 2006. Reprinted by permission.

As you read, consider the following questions:

1. According to the author, why have the media failed to place methadone overdoses in context?

2. Why is OxyContin a "revolutionary drug," in Szalavitz's view?

3. Why are OxyContin and methadone generally safe when prescribed, as stated by Szalavitz?

Meth, we hardly knew you; say howdy to methadone—the new demon drug according to the media, who—oops—helped turn it into a hazard.

Looks like there's a new demon drug on the block—the opioid painkiller methadone, which is also commonly used as a substitute therapy to treat people addicted to heroin or prescription painkillers. But as usual with drugs coverage, the press doesn't recognize its own responsibility in the devil's creation.

Recently, media ranging from the *Birmingham News* to ABC's *20/20* have noted increased numbers of methadone overdose deaths.

But what they haven't done is put the story in context. While the coverage is careful to say that most methadone on the street is not being diverted from the clinics that use it to treat addicts, it usually claims that, as the *Birmingham News* put it by citing a police source, "the drug is being prescribed more often to help people treat pain than to control addiction. As the prescriptions have increased, so have instances of abuse."

However, these stories fail to note the reason why methadone prescriptions for pain treatment have increased. In the early [20]00s, the media went into a feeding frenzy over a new deadly painkiller, OxyContin, which was supposedly addicting countless young people and causing record numbers of overdose deaths in rural areas. The drug became known as "hillbilly heroin," and once there was a clever name for it, the hype express took off.

Even though skeptics rapidly discovered that the death rates and new addiction rates had been exaggerated, and even though stories about people "accidentally addicted" by doctors turned out in the main to be stories of addicts scamming doctors to get drugs, OxyContin kept its bad name. And as the DEA [US Drug Enforcement Administration] started a new initiative to fight prescription drug abuse focused on ending the "Oxy" menace, physicians became much more cautious about prescribing it.

With the DEA looking closely at OxyContin prescriptions and with no decline in the number of pain patients, doctors began to look for alternatives. OxyContin had been a revolutionary drug because if it is used appropriately (not ground up and made into a short-acting drug as addicts do with it), it provides 12 hours of pain relief, compared to four to six hours for other drugs.

Driving Doctors to a More Dangerous Drug

An older, cheaper drug also provides lasting relief, and yes, it's called methadone. It has long been used as a "maintenance" treatment for addicts precisely because it is the opioid drug which has the greatest staying power (only a derivative, LAAM [levacetylmethadol] lasts longer).

Methadone's effects persist for 24–48 hours. Contrary to popular belief, the longer a high lasts, the less addictive it is. This is part of why crack is more addictive than powder cocaine and why ground-up OxyContin is more addictive than OxyContin taken as directed (and yes, it means, too, that crack is more addictive than methamphetamine, contrary to media claims that longer-acting drugs are more attractive to addicts).

65

Once a user is tolerant to opioids, they produce no high and—with longer-acting drugs—none of the "ups and downs" associated with addiction, thereby allowing people to function normally. Such users are not cognitively, emotionally or physically impaired and can drive safely on doses that would incapacitate the non-tolerant. The same is true for people who take these drugs for pain.

But long-acting drugs are a double-edged sword: If there are going to be adverse effects, they may not appear immediately. Because neither OxyContin nor methadone is intended to be given to patients who are not already tolerant to other opioids, they are generally very safe when taken by such people as prescribed.

Methadone, however, is less safe than OxyContin because of the extreme length of its action. Pain patients or street users unfamiliar with this effect may believe the drug has worn off long before it has—and the result can be overdose. Doctors unfamiliar with prescribing the drug can inadvertently lead patients to overdose as well; an investigation by a Charleston paper noted that the prescribing information packaged with the drug may mislead doctors about safe doses for those who are not tolerant to opioids.

So, by hyping the dangers of OxyContin, the media have actually driven doctors to use a more dangerous drug. And by hyping the dangers of methadone without putting them in context, [the media are] failing to acknowledge the larger story and failing to give readers and viewers the accurate information they need to understand the complexities of pain treatment and addiction.

Periodical and Internet Sources Bibliography

The following articles have been selected to supplement the diverse views presented in this chapter.

Johannah Cornblatt	"More States Ban Salvia," *U.S. News & World Report*, July 18 2008.
Meghan Daum	"Long, Strange Trip to Ecstasy," *Los Angeles Times*, May 3, 2008.
Lee Erica Elder	"Mean Green: Salvia: A Look at the Unknown Risks of This Powerful Drug," *Current Health 2, a Weekly Reader Publication*, December 2009.
Victoria Stagg Elliott	"Altering Perceptions: Good Outcomes from 'Club Drugs?'" *American Medical News*, October 1, 2007.
Richard Maffeo	"Drugs' Deadly Kid-Friendly Face: Is That Really a Sweet Tart?" *Vibrant Life*, November 2006.
Mike Males	"This Is Your Brain on Drugs, Dad," *New York Times*, January 3, 2007.
Philip Nobile	"Studio 54, Where Are You?" *New York*, May 7, 2007.
Science World	"Real Questions, Real Answers: Leading Scientists Give Teens the Facts About Drug Abuse," November 9, 2009.
Melissa Walker	"A Prescription for Addiction," *Girls' Life*, April–May 2009.

OPPOSING
VIEWPOINTS®
SERIES

CHAPTER 2

What Causes Chemical Dependency?

Chapter Preface

Drug use without medical supervision or a prescription to produce a therapeutic effect is called self-medication. While this includes taking over-the-counter drugs to ease a cold, it's also a recognized theory of drug addiction, according to researchers Edward J. Khantzian and Mark J. Albanese, who are longtime proponents of the hypothesis. "First, addictive drugs become addicting because they have the powerful effect of alleviating, removing, or changing human psychological suffering," Khantzian and Albanese write in their 2008 book *Understanding Addiction as Self Medication: Finding Hope Behind the Pain.* "A second important aspect is that there is a considerable degree of specificity in a person's drug of choice. Addictive drugs are not universally appealing," the authors continue. "Although a person might experiment and use a number of addictive substances, individuals navigate toward a certain drug because of what it does for them." These addicts, Khantzian and Albanese suggest, may have suffered from physical abuse, sexual violence, or some other traumatizing event, and experience difficulty in controlling their emotions. "Emotions are experienced in the extreme; they are either overwhelming or numbing or confusing. It should not be surprising that an opiate would calm the agitation associated with this condition, as it would an obliterating dose of alcohol, or that cocaine or crystal methamphetamine would alter or relieve the numbing, empty feeling states," they maintain.

In a review of *Understanding Addiction as Self Medication,* Bryon Adinoff, a professor in Drug and Alcohol Abuse Research at the University of Texas Southwestern Medical Center, questions the self-medication theory in the context of other underlying factors. "Not mentioned is the extensive literature revealing a complex of genetic, behavioral, and environmental factors that increase the risk of substance use in at-risk youths but do not predict a specific drug of use,"[1] he contends. "It would have been a powerful argument, for example, if the authors had offered a biologic foundation for the effects of specific drugs on identified affect states." In the following viewpoints, the authors argue for and against the numerous scientific, medical, and psychological explanations for drug addiction.

1. *American Journal of Psychiatry*, November 2009. http://ajp.psychiatryonline.org.

> *"Addictive substances hijack the brain's reward system, weakening our resolve to make wise choices even when painful consequences are sure to result."*

Addiction Is a Brain Disease

Michael Craig Miller

Michael Craig Miller is editor in chief of the Harvard Mental Health Letter. *In the following viewpoint, Miller states that more than 20 million Americans deal with addiction. Addiction is not a result of a person's flawed character, but rather of distorted brain function. Addictive substances such as cocaine weaken a person's ability to make wise choices by taking control of the brain's reward system. Scientists are gaining understanding in how addiction can change the brain, which is resulting in treatments for the brain disease.*

As you read, consider the following questions:

1. What "chemical messenger" do addictive substances release into the nucleus accumbens of the brain?

2. As stated in the viewpoint, what is the name of the archetype compound that reverses the pleasurable result of narcotics?

3. According to Miller, what combination of treatments works best when dealing with addiction?

Remember "Just say no"? It was a slick motto, but a terrible remedy for drug and alcohol dependence. Decades later, more than 20 million Americans are still wrestling with addiction. This disease costs the nation almost $500 billion a year—more than diabetes and cancer combined. The problem is not flawed character; it's skewed brain function. Fortunately, scientists are now well on their way to understanding how addiction changes the brain, and this knowledge is starting to yield treatments that work.

Addictive substances hijack the brain's reward system, weakening our resolve to make wise choices even when painful consequences are sure to result. Specifically, they stimulate the release of the chemical messenger dopamine into a region of the brain called the nucleus accumbens. Cocaine and other stimulants cause this change directly. Other substances—alcohol, narcotics, nicotine and marijuana—act indirectly. But in each case, the sensation is self-reinforcing. Feel it once and you want to feel it again.

This common pathway begs for a magic-bullet treatment, but the cycle of addiction is actually more complicated. It involves multiple chemical messengers, not just dopamine. The good news is that each of these messengers offers a possible target for treatment, and researchers are taking aim at them. The clearest recent advance is a new group of medications that work to combat craving. The archetype, a compound called naltrexone, reverses the pleasurable effect of narcotics like heroin. It also slows the release of dopamine in the nucleus accumbens. Recovering alcoholics tend to experience less euphoria when they drink while taking naltrexone, and their chances of staying in recovery improve. But the drug is far from curative. It doesn't completely extinguish the desire to drink, and people who lack counseling and support often have trouble taking it every day. A new long-acting form of naltrexone could reach the clinic next year [2006], enabling patients to get a month's worth of treatment in a single injection.

That's just the beginning. Last year the FDA [Food and Drug Administration] approved a drug called acamprosate, which reduces craving by slowing the release of the chemical messenger glutamate. Some experts are also hopeful about topiramate, a migraine and seizure drug that boosts a signaling substance called GABA (gamma-aminobutyric acid). Yet another candidate is ondansetron, a serotonin blocker used to treat nausea in cancer patients. Studies suggest it can help cut alcohol consumption in people who take up drinking early in life.

Who Gets Addicted

While pursuing better treatments, researchers are also tackling the question of who gets addicted, and why. Heredity leaves some of us more addiction prone than others, possibly because we metabolize drugs at different rates or respond more strongly to their effects. The research suggests that genetic differences may also affect our responses to treatment. A few studies have found that patients with a family history of alcoholism are more responsive to naltrexone than people without a family history. In a recent study, patients who had a gene variant dubbed Asp40 got more benefit from naltrexone than those with a different version of the gene. Markers like these, once better established, will help doctors figure out which treatments are best for individual patients.

We're still a long way from pills that will make treatment easy. Long-term strategies are essential even when medication works because the affected brain circuits don't return to normal right away, if ever. We now know that treatments combining medication and psychotherapy work better than either strategy does by itself. Next year, an eight-year study called COMBINE (Combining Medications and Behavioral Interventions) will provide the best evidence yet on how to weave drugs and therapy into a comprehensive treatment plan. Bitter experience may temper our hopes. But if we can finally begin to understand this illness instead of demonizing the victims, we may come up with approaches that help.

> "Similarities between serious substance
> dependence and other chronic illnesses
> are striking."

Addiction Is a Chronic Disorder

William L. White and Thomas McClellan

In the following viewpoint, William L. White and Thomas Mc-Clellan propose that drug addiction has the main features of a chronic disease. First, the authors state that the symptoms of addiction can be treated, but the root causes cannot. Second, treatment of addiction requires major lifestyle and behavioral changes to optimize the benefits. Third, the authors insist that relapses are a part of addiction, and recovering addicts require consistent monitoring and support of medical professionals and family to sustain a sober, healthy way of life. White is a senior research consultant at Chestnut Health Systems and the author of Slaying the Dragon: The History of Addiction Treatment and Recovery in America. *McClellan is a professor of psychiatry at the University of Pennsylvania and founder and executive director of the Treatment Research Institute in Philadelphia.*

William L. White and Thomas McClellan, "Addiction as a Chronic Disorder," *Counselor Magazine*, July 2008. Copyright © 2008 by Health Communications, Inc. Reprinted with the permissions of the publishers, www.hcibooks.com

As you read, consider the following questions:

1. What are the two major implications of addiction as a chronic disease, in the authors' opinion?

2. Why is the perception of addiction as a chronic disease problematic among the public, in White and McClellan's view?

3. What is the authors' position on recovery processes?

Modern medicine has recognized that chronic diseases cannot and should not be treated and managed like acute disorders.

Acute disorders such as bacterial infections, broken bones and even emotional trauma from shock or injury can typically be traced to a clearly identifiable source (e.g., an infectious agent, physical trauma) and can be "cured" through treatment and recovery processes that span a relatively short period of time. The onset, course and resolution of acute disorders may be intense and disruptive, but they generally leave no lasting mark on one's identity or functional capabilities. The treatment process essentially returns the body to its original state— the treated individual is no more (or less) susceptible to a return of the disease or condition than an individual who never had the disease. Thus, while a treated individual may again break a bone or get another infection, this is considered a new occurrence and not a relapse. In contrast, chronic diseases such as diabetes, asthma or heart disease spring from and are complicated by, multiple biological, psychological and social factors, some of which cannot be clearly identified. Many times "lifestyle" or personal behavioral choices are intimately involved in the onset and course of these disorders. While there are usually several potentially effective treatments for chronic disorders, they are of necessity more complex and protracted than acute treatments, and they do not produce the same kinds of outcomes as acute treatments.

Main Features of Chronic Disorders

All chronic treatments, regardless of disease, share three important features. First, they can usually remove or reduce the symptoms of the disease, but cannot affect the root causes of the disease. For example, beta blockers reduce blood pressure and insulin improves the body's ability to digest sugars and starches, as long as the affected individual continues the treatment. However, these treatments do not return the affected individual to normal.

The second feature associated with all chronic treatments is that they require significant changes in lifestyle and behavior on the part of the patient to maximize their benefit. Again, even if individuals with diabetes regularly take their insulin as prescribed, this will not stop disease progression if they do not also reduce sugar and starch intake, increase exercise and reduce stress levels.

The third feature derives from the first two. Because of the complexity of factors that can lead to a chronic illness and because of the need for ongoing medical care and lifestyle change, it should not be surprising that relapses are very likely to occur in all chronic illnesses. For these reasons, most contemporary treatment strategies in chronic illness involve regular in-person and/or telephone monitoring of medication adherence, coupled with encouragement and support for pro-health changes in diet, exercise and stress levels. Increasingly, family members are being trained to also provide continued monitoring and support for the behavioral changes necessary to maintain symptom remission and sustain good quality of life.

As is evident from this short preface, the onset and course of chronic illnesses are not like those of acute illnesses; and for these reasons chronic care has to be quite different from acute care. While many in our field have come to consider some (not all) forms of addiction as chronic, this change in thinking has not been followed by changes in treatment strategy, monitoring methods, insurance coverage or outcome expectations. With this as background, [this viewpoint]: 1) summarizes the history of the conceptualization of severe alcohol and other drug dependence as a chronic disease; 2) updates the scientific evidence comparing alcohol and drug dependence to diabetes mellitus, hypertension and asthma; and 3) identifies the central messages that addiction professionals can communicate to clients, families and referral sources regarding addiction treatment and long-term recovery management strategies.

Historical Background

The earliest conceptualizations of chronic drunkenness as a medical condition by Drs. Benjamin Rush and Thomas Trotter were followed by more substantive treatises by Drs. M. Huss, W. Marcet, T.D. Crothers and others, all of whom noted the prolonged course of alcohol dependence and the professional challenges involved in its treatment. The origins of terms such as habituation, inebriety, dipsomania, alcoholism and addiction were rooted in efforts to convey a condition far more complex and enduring than the threat posed by an episode of acute alcohol or other drug intoxication. The recognition of the chronicity and complexity of severe alcohol and other drug problems led to the calls for special institutions for the care of the inebriate and the subsequent birth of inebriate homes, inebriate asylums and private addiction cure institutes.

There were several early pioneers who suggested that the treatment of addiction should mirror the treatment of other chronic diseases. In 1828, Dr. J.H. Kain penned an essay on the treatment of intemperance in which he invoked the medical maxim, "chronic diseases require chronic cures." Dr. T.D. Crothers expressed similar sentiments in an 1879 editorial in the *Journal of Inebriety*:

> The permanent cure of inebriates under treatment in asylums will compare favorably in numbers with that of any

other disease of the nervous system which is more or less chronic before the treatment is commenced.

Such comparisons of addiction to other chronic disorders were lost in the larger collapse of the inebriate asylum movement in the opening decades of the twentieth century.

As interest in alcoholism as a public health problem arose again in the mid-twentieth century, alcoholism was again compared to other chronic diseases. A 1938 report of the Scientific Committee of the Research Council on Problems of Alcohol concluded, "An alcoholic should be regarded as a sick person, just as one who is suffering from tuberculosis, cancer, heart disease, or other serious chronic disorder." Also worthy of note is a 1947 article by Dr. R.E. Duncan published in the *Kansas City Medical Journal*. Duncan declared that alcoholism is a "chronic affair" and that "chronic conditions must be approached on a long-range basis." He further concluded, that to foster complete recovery, treatment must be continued for years after the patient has been sobered.

Duncan was one of the first practitioners to explore the full clinical implications of the chronicity of addiction. During this same period, [S.] Charles Franco, an early industrial alcoholism pioneer, wrote a 1951 article "Chronic Alcoholism as a Medical Problem in Industry." He called for recognizing alcoholism "as much a disease as diabetes or tuberculosis." . . .

Treatment in an Acute Care Model

The emphasis on alcoholism as a chronic disease was lost in the larger battle to convey to the American public and policy makers that alcoholism was a disease. This effort spanned the 1940s to 1960s and led to landmark legislation in 1970 that set the stage for the rise of community-based, time-limited addiction treatment in the United States. This was followed by a rapid process of professionalization and commercialization and subsequent emergence of an aggressive system of managed behavioral health care in the United States. Despite (or perhaps because of) these forces, nearly all modalities of addiction treatment migrated toward an acute care (AC) model of intervention—even traditionally long-term modalities such as therapeutic communities and methadone maintenance. The AC model is characterized by the following central elements:

- Services are delivered "programmatically" in a uniform series of encapsulated activities (screening, admission, a single point-in-time assessment, treatment procedures, discharge, and brief "after care" followed by termination of the service relationship).

- A professional expert directs and dominates the assessment, treatment planning and service delivery decision making throughout this process.

- Services transpire over a short (and historically ever-shorter) period of time, usually as a function of pre-arranged, time-limited insurance payments designed specifically for addiction disorders and "carved out" from general medical insurance.

- The individual/family/community is given the impression at discharge ("graduation") that "cure has occurred": long-term recovery is now self-sustainable without ongoing professional assistance.

- Post-treatment relapse and readmissions are viewed as the failure (noncompliance) of the individual rather than potential flaws in the design or execution of the treatment protocol.

By the later 1990s, the assumptions of the AC model began to be questioned. These early critiques were followed by widespread calls to extend the design of addiction treatment from an AC model to a model of sustained recovery management. One call to redesign addiction treatment was the publication of "Drug Dependence, a Chronic Medical Illness" in the *Journal of the American Medical Association*. In the next section, we summarize and update the major findings of this seminal article.

Addiction as a Chronic Medical Illness

It is important to state at the outset that not all alcohol- and other drug-related (AOD) problems inevitably become chronic disorders; and that clinical research has not yet been able to clearly predict which early cases will ultimately become chronic. Many substance use problems are developmental and as such are often outgrown in the successful transition from adolescence into adulthood. Others occur in tandem with major life transitions (e.g., death of a loved one, divorce, job loss) and are resolved by time, natural support, brief professional intervention or peer-based intervention by others in recovery. Similarly, many of those who experience a period of high blood pressure will essentially get over this problem through change of lifestyle, loss of weight and increased physical activity. It is not currently possible to predict who will go on to develop chronic hypertension.

For many reasons, most of those entering addiction treatment are characterized by greater personal vulnerability for AOD problems (e.g., family history of AOD problems, early onset of AOD use, traumatic victimization); greater problem severity (e.g., substance dependence); greater problem complexity (e.g., concurrent medical/psychiatric illness, multiple drug use); and fewer personal and family resources to initiate and sustain a long-term recovery process. There are striking similarities between substance dependence as seen in the clinical setting and other chronic illnesses such as [type] 2 diabetes mellitus, hypertension and asthma. Severe substance dependence and these other primary chronic illnesses:

- Are influenced by genetic heritability and other personal, family and environmental risk factors.

81

- Can be identified and diagnosed using well-validated screening questionnaires and diagnostic checklists.

- Are influenced by behaviors that begin as voluntary choices but evolve into deeply ingrained patterns of behavior that, in the case of addiction, are further exacerbated by neurobiological changes in the brain that weaken volitional control over these contributing behaviors.

- Are marked by a pattern of onset that may be sudden or gradual.

- Have a prolonged course that varies from person to person in intensity and pattern.

- Are accompanied by risks of profound pathophysiology, disability and premature death.

- Have effective treatments, self-management protocols, peer support frameworks and similar remission rates, but no known cures.

These similarities between serious substance dependence and other chronic illnesses are striking. It is important to note that even substantial similarity does not mean that similar disease processes are at work across these conditions. However, at the very least, the similarities argue for consideration of the same kinds of chronic or continuing care strategies for alcohol and drug dependence that have been employed in other chronic diseases. If substance dependence is like other chronic illnesses, then this raises two important implications: 1) acute care models of intervention for severe substance dependence may reduce substance use temporarily but those reductions are not likely to sustain once care stops; and 2) methods used in the treatment of other chronic illnesses might be effectively adapted to enhance long-term recovery from substance dependence. These implications offer an explanation of the generally high and rapid rates of relapse following cessation of most available addiction treatments: There is simply no quick fix for the most severe forms of this disorder. . . .

Communicating About Addiction as a Chronic Disease

Many communications about addiction, and especially communications comparing it to other chronic illnesses, can arouse strong feelings and unintended, harmful implications. Because of the significant family and social problems associated with addictive disorders, strong feelings are aroused when these conditions are discussed as "illnesses" or "chronic diseases." To many in the public at large this represents inappropriate "medicalization"; abrogation of personal responsibility for those affected; and a ready-made excuse for ineffective treatment for the treatment field. Perhaps worse, many individuals with substance use disorders who have gained and maintained recovery may resent the idea that they have a "continuing chronic illness."

Thus, care must be taken in how the chronic nature of addiction is communicated to the policy makers and the public, clients, family members, referral sources and to those working on the front lines of addiction treatment. In the service of better communication we first discuss what this concept of addiction as a chronic illness does NOT imply; followed by 10 concepts and correlates that may be helpful in thinking about and discussing appropriate and effective continuing care for chronic forms of this illness.

Things NOT Implied or Suggested by the Concept of Addiction as a Chronic Illness

- All AOD problems are NOT chronic, most do NOT have a prolonged and progressive course; some do, and research is needed to identify early signs of chronic progression.

- All persons with AOD problems do NOT need special-ized, professional, long-term monitoring and support—many recover on their own, with family or peer support; again, research is needed to identify who is most likely to need intensive, professional care.

- Among those who do need treatment, relapse is NOT inevitable and all persons suffering from substance de-pendence do NOT require multiple treatments before they achieve stable, long-term recovery.

- Even among those who do relapse following treatment, families, friends and employers should NOT abandon hope for recovery. (Community studies of recovery from alcohol dependence report long-term recovery rates approaching or exceeding 50 percent.)

- Having the serious chronic illness of addiction, DOES NOT reduce personal responsibility for continuous ef-forts to manage that illness, just as those with serious diabetes or hypertensive disease must also manage their illnesses.

- Appropriate treatment for chronic addiction is NOT simply a succession of short-term detoxifications or treatment stays. Appropriate continuing care requires personal commitment to long-term change, dedication to self-management, community and family support and monitoring.

- Current addiction treatment outcomes are NOT accept-able simply because they are comparable to those achieved with other chronic disorders.

Things That ARE Important in Considering the Concept of Addiction as a Chronic Illness

- Chronic diseases vary. Not everyone at risk for a chronic disease contracts the disease or experiences the same course of the disease. Chronic diseases exhibit a high degree of variability in pattern of onset, course and intensity (self-accelerating, constant, alternating cycles of remission and relapse or decelerating). Each case of chronic disease varies in physiological severity, functional impairment and the financial/emotional burden placed on the individual, family and society. The course of chronic disorders is influenced by the interaction of such factors as type and degree of biological vulnerability, age of onset, problem severity, problem complexity (e.g., presence of co-occurring disorders) and degree of individual, family and community recovery capital (assets that can be drawn upon to initiate and sustain recovery). Adding to the burden of chronic disorders is their propensity to beget other acute and chronic disorders such as depression and chronic pain.

- Chronic diseases require prolonged and active management. Chronic disorders require strategic, sustained stewardship of personal, family and community resources. Core strategies for achieving long-term recovery from chronic disorders include: stabilization of active episodes; global assessment; enhancement of global health; sustained professional monitoring and early re-intervention; continuity of contact in a primary recovery support relationship; and development of a peer-based recovery support network. Choices for the treatment and management of chronic disorders diminish through disease progression and expand with sustained stabilization and enhancements in global health.

- Both full and partial recoveries are possible. There are permanent solutions to severe alcohol and other drug problems. Millions of individuals and families throughout the world live full lives in long-term recovery from these problems. Their increasingly public stories, even

more than the accumulation of scientific studies, offer
living proof of this proposition. Partial recoveries are
also possible. An essential strategy of chronic disease
management is optimizing personal functioning and
quality of life even after abstinence has been achieved.
Recovery management strategies for persons with the
most severe and persistent disorders include multiple
goals: reducing the number, intensity and duration of
relapse episodes; strengthening and extending the
length of remission periods; reducing the personal and
social costs associated with relapse; reducing the propensity for drug substitution and other excessive behaviors during early periods of recovery initiation; and
enhancing the quality of personal/family life through
both the remission and relapse phases of the disorder.
Partial recovery may constitute a prelude to resumed
substance dependence, a permanent state, or a stage of
ambivalence and instability that precedes the achieve-
ment of full recovery.

- Recovery processes vary. There are multiple pathways,
patterns and personal styles of long-term recovery. The
time and resources required to fully resolve alcohol and
other drug problems vary from individual to individual. Greater time and resources are often required as
substance use disorders become more severe and complex and as personal, family and community recovery
capital diminish. Beyond this general guideline, there is
no way to predict who will sustain recovery following a
single effort, who will achieve recovery after multiple
efforts or who will fail to achieve recovery.

- Lapses after recovery initiation are common but not
inevitable. A lapse (episode of alcohol or drug use) or
relapse (resumption of compulsive use and its related
problems) following treatment does not mean that

there is no hope for recovery. A significant portion of persons currently in long-term recovery experienced one or more lapse/relapse episodes before achieving sustainable sobriety. Such events do call for renewed intervention, a refinement in strategies of recovery maintenance and greater resources for long-term support.

• Natural support matters. The prospects of long-term recovery for individuals are enhanced by sustained family and social support. Family members and friends can take concerted action to shorten a loved one's addiction career (the span of time from problem onset to stable recovery maintenance) and to enhance the health of all family members and the family unit.

• Intervening early makes a difference. Recognizing and intervening in the alcohol and other drug problems of a family member can shorten his or her addiction career. There are brief windows of opportunity within the course of addiction that can be capitalized upon to help initiate and solidify long-term recovery.

• Personal and family recovery take time. Some of the personal/family problems that preceded or developed after the onset of alcohol and other drug problems continue into the early years of recovery. The resolution of these problems requires time, sustained effort and quite often, professional help.

• Professional and peer support helps. Individual and family recoveries are enhanced by sustained professional and peer support. Monitoring the status of a chronic disease, the effectiveness of the efforts to manage it, and changing physical, psychological, behavioral and environmental risk factors are crucial elements in chronic disease management. Sustained participation in peer-based recovery support groups and other recovery community institutions (e.g., recovery homes, recovery schools, recovery ministries) can elevate long-term recovery rates. Primary physicians, addiction professionals and other frontline health care providers constitute an important resource for long-term recovery checkups and support.

• Recovery is a marathon that can bring unexpected gifts. Recovery from severe alcohol and other drug problems, like recovery from other primary health problems such as diabetes, asthma or heart disease, requires sustained vigilance and effort. Recovery gives back to individuals and families what was taken through the addiction process. Some individuals and families will be stronger, healthier and live more personally meaningful and fulfilled lives as a result of their shared recovery experience.

A Historical Opportunity

Reengineering addiction treatment into a system of sustained recovery support will be both a major challenge and an important opportunity for society. We invite those on the front lines of addiction treatment to join us in writing this new future for addiction recovery in America.

| "*Addiction is voluntary rather than compulsory.*"

Addiction Is Not a Disease

Gene M. Heyman, as told to Daniel Akst

Gene M. Heyman is a research psychologist at McLean Hospital and author of Addiction: A Disorder of Choice. *Daniel Akst is a writer based in New York's Hudson Valley. In the following viewpoint, Heyman opposes the disease model of drug addiction. He puts forth that the majority of addicts quit without professional help due to factors such as family relationships and finances, which do not end chronic diseases like schizophrenia and Alzheimer's disease. Furthermore, while Heyman does not dispute the hereditary component of dependency, he proposes that incentives of costs and benefits matter more in decision making. The fact that addiction is not a disease is encouraging and helpful, he argues.*

As you read, consider the following questions:

1. How does Heyman back his claim that most addicts quit without medical intervention?

2. Why is the disease model of addiction prevalent, in Heyman's opinion?

3. How can drug treatment programs be more effective, according to Heyman?

For years, the enlightened—and widely held—view of addiction has been that it is a disease. Chronic drug abusers, for example, are physiologically compelled to continue their self-destructive behavior. They often have a genetic predisposition toward addiction, and their drug abuse results in biochemical changes in the body. Addicts need help if they are to be saved.

But in a new book from Harvard University Press, the psychologist Gene M. Heyman says this conventional wisdom is wrong. *Addiction: a Disorder of Choice* makes the provocative argument that addiction is voluntary rather than compulsory, that addicts respond to incentives just like most other people, and that in fact most drug addicts stop "using" without the help of treatment.

Heyman's book, which seems likely to generate controversy, argues that all choices, including drug dependence, are influenced by preferences and goals. Addicts tend to quit when adult responsibilities weigh more heavily, and the costs of addiction (financial, marital, and otherwise) become greater than the benefits. Humans, in Heyman's view, have an innate tendency to overconsume the things they like best because of our great susceptibility to short-term rewards—even if those rewards happen to be harmful in the long term.

Addiction, Heyman notes, remains widely seen as a "chronic, relapsing brain disease," yet unlike most other supposed diseases you can be imprisoned for it (if you're caught with illegal drugs). But "medical treatment and punishment," the author says, "do not exhaust the possible responses to human problems." Finding suitable alternatives is one reason it matters whether or not addiction is in fact an illness.

The author is a research psychologist at McLean Hospital and a lecturer at Harvard, from which he earned a PhD. He is also an adjunct associate professor at Boston College. . . .

Volunteering to Be an Addict?

Daniel Akst: What's the evidence that addiction is in fact voluntary? And why would anyone volunteer to be addicted?

Gene M. Heyman: The American Psychiatric Association and World Health Organization describe addiction as a form of involuntary, compulsive drug use. The American National Institute on Drug Abuse describes addiction as a chronic, relapsing disease. I tested these claims by asking whether addicts typically remain long-term drug users, and what, if anything, helps them to stop using drugs. Every national survey of psychiatric disorders has revealed that most addicts were actually ex-addicts. The quit rate was about 75 percent. According to the age statistics, most addicts had quit using drugs at clinically significant levels by about 30 to 35 years old.

The surveys also reveal that most addicts, typically over 70 percent, did not seek clinical help. So they must have quit without professional assistance. In-depth interviews showed that quitting was preceded by such factors as the drug user's concern about finances, desire for respect from family, keeping or getting a job, and worries about health. In other words, the usual factors that influence everyday decisions helped addicts quit drugs.

But those same factors do not eliminate the symptoms of schizophrenia or Alzheimer's disease. Accordingly, we call these disorders "diseases." I do not mean to say that someone chooses to be an addict. Rather, they choose to have just one more drink or quit tomorrow. A long enough series of one-more-times makes an addict. Addicts tend to quit when the "hassles" of maintaining their habit become too great (sometimes called "hitting bottom").

How is it that no one has noticed these studies and other factors before? Is there some reason we are so wedded to the disease model?

First, the recovery numbers are buried in tables and presented in ways that obscure the quit rates. Although the math is simple, readers have to calculate the quit rates for themselves. Second, most research is based on addicts who come to clinics. But these are a distinct minority, and they are much more likely to keep using drugs past the age of 30—probably because they have many more health problems than nonclinic addicts. They are about twice as likely to suffer from depression, and are many times more likely to have HIV/AIDS. These problems interfere with activities that can successfully compete with drug use. Thus, experts have based their view of addiction on an unrepresentative sample of addicts.

Also, if we recognize that addiction is voluntary then we have to conclude that individuals are quite capable of voluntary self-destructive behavior. This is hard to understand, and it raises questions about the wisdom of forms of government and economic institutions that assume human rationality—that individuals make choices which favor their best long-term interests. Addiction tells us that humans can act persistently against their own interests. Novelists and dramatists know this, but it's an idea that doesn't easily fit the modern scientific viewpoint.

Incentives Matter

But doesn't addiction have a strong hereditary component?

Yes. We are biological creatures, and even voluntary behavior has a biology, including a genetic background. The question is not whether addiction has a biological basis—it does—but whether its biological basis prevents drug use from coming under the influence of costs and benefits. As it turns out, incentives matter.

What about the claim that addictive substances (which these days are said to include food, the Internet, and all kinds of other things) cause changes in the brain that make it almost impossible to exercise restraint?

All experience that changes behavior does so by changing the brain. The critical question is whether these changes are deleterious, and whether they block the influence of the fac-

Smoking Is Not Cancer

Addiction is not a disease. It is not something someone has. It is not a lesion, or a seizure. Addiction is not involuntary. This distinction is important because since addiction is not a disease, it can be neither diagnosed nor treated.

Despite the fact that behavior and disease are different, many people who believe addiction is "treatable" equate the two. Smoking is a behavior. Cancer is a disease. Drinking is a behavior. Cirrhosis of the liver is a disease. Smoking is not cancer. Drinking is not cirrhosis.

Jeffrey A. Schaler,
"Internet Addiction: To Diagnose or Disregard,"
New Therapist, *May/June 2000.*

tors that support self-control. My hunch is that if drug-induced brain changes do not block the influence of costs and benefits on drug use, then Internet-induced brain changes do not make turning off your computer impossible.

If addiction is not a disease, what should we do differently to help one another and ourselves?

I do not pretend to be a policy expert. But the implication of my analysis is that drug prevention and treatment programs should focus on things that raise the value of nondrug activities and lower the value of drugs. This could include pharmacological methods such as methadone, which block the pleasure of heroin, and training that provides high-risk populations with marketable skills. Schooling is worth emphasizing, since educational attainment is the strongest predictor of avoiding drug problems. Just publicizing the fact that most addicts quit—and that addiction is not a chronic disease—may be helpful. It's encouraging news, and it has the advantage of being true.

"Specific experiences combine with genetic factors to slick the road to addiction."

Addiction Is Caused by Genetic and Environmental Factors

Claudia Wallis

In the following viewpoint, Claudia Wallis writes that genetic variations, personal background, and social factors can shape how one reacts to drug and alcohol use, including becoming addicted. Large-scale studies with twins, she says, prove that addiction is one of the most inherited mental illnesses. Willis also maintains that subsets of the population handle the ill effects of certain drugs or drinking differently, affecting likelihoods of dependency. Paired with genetic traits, childhood trauma and abuse can predispose a person to addictive behavior, Wallis concludes. Wallis is editor at large at Time.

As you read, consider the following questions:

1. How does David Goldman compare crack addiction to pot smoking?

Claudia Wallis, "The Genetics of Addiction," CNNMoney.com, October 16, 2009. Reprinted by permission.

2. In Wallis's words, how is alcohol tolerance determined in chromosomes?

3. How does Wallis back her assertion that genetics and abuse are factors in chemical dependency?

Why do some people get hooked on drugs and alcohol, while others can party hard and walk away? We tend to think it's a matter of willpower or moral fiber, but it has more to do with a roll of the genetic dice.

Large-scale studies of twins provide strong evidence that addiction ranks "among the most heritable of mental illnesses," says Dr. David Goldman, who heads the Laboratory of Neurogenetics at the National Institute on Alcohol Abuse and Alcoholism.

Of course, personal experience and social influences matter, too. Addiction researchers like Goldman have begun to pinpoint how specific experiences combine with genetic factors to slick the road to addiction.

Numerous genes have been linked to addiction, though fewer than a dozen have been strongly implicated.

Some are substance specific, for example, genetic variations that influence the metabolism of alcohol. Some relate to mood, anxiety, and personality disorders, which are often present in people who seek solace or stimulation in alcohol or drugs. Some gene patterns are involved in more than one type of addiction, perhaps influencing brain pathways involved in seeking rewards.

"If you have a twin who uses cocaine, it makes you more likely to use heroin. If you have a twin who uses tobacco, you are more likely to use alcohol," Goldman explains.

Even the tendency to try a dangerous, illegal drug like crack or heroin is partially under genetic control. For instance, an area on chromosome 11, associated with taking risks and seeking novel experiences, lies near a region that has been linked to addiction.

Researchers use animal studies to measure the addictive tug of a particular drug. Marijuana and hallucinogens are not very habit forming, while cocaine and opiates are so compelling that lab rats prefer them to food.

What's interesting, says Goldman, is that the more addictive the substance, the stronger the role of heredity in causing an addiction to it. Thus, he explains, while genetics strongly influence your risk of becoming a crack addict, becoming a pothead has more to do with social factors like "whether you like rolling joints or the company of other marijuana users."

As every social drinker or pot smoker knows, individuals vary markedly in their response to substances. Much of this is genetically determined and it has big implications for who gets hooked.

Some folks can't handle opiates, notes Goldman; even a medicinal dose of codeine makes them feel sick. Responses to alcohol also vary enormously. Some people literally get a bigger kick out of champagne, because alcohol provides a bigger boost to their endorphin levels—a difference that has been mapped to variations in opiate receptor genes.

Differences in how well people handle the ill effects of drinking—nausea, dizziness, and so on—are also under genetic control—and influence the risk of addiction.

In both animals and humans, individuals who are less sensitive to these unpleasant effects have a higher rate of addiction. Regions on chromosomes 4 and 5 that govern the neurotransmitter GABA [gamma-aminobutyric acid] appear to play a key role in determining alcohol tolerance.

On the other hand, two genes that are common in Asian populations—present in about 36% of Chinese, Japanese, and Koreans—cause people to turn red in the face and develop a rapid heartbeat and nausea when they drink.

The phenomenon, sometimes called "Asian glow" or "Asian flush" is due to a buildup of a nasty alcohol byproduct called acetaldehyde, a chemical cousin of the preservative formaldehyde. (The anti-drinking drug Antabuse works the same way.)

People with genes for this unpleasant flushing syndrome are, of course, less likely to develop a drinking problem. Those who drink anyway are putting themselves in peril. Recent research shows that they have a high risk of developing deadly esophageal cancer. For the half a billion people who carry these genes, concludes Goldman, "alcohol is now identified as a carcinogen."

But genes alone do not cause an addiction. Researchers like to point out that, as with other ailments linked to lifestyle—heart disease, obesity, and lung cancer, for example—genes merely load the gun, while the environment pulls the trigger.

New studies are beginning to reveal precisely how this can work. For example, women who were abused as children are known to have high rates of alcoholism and yet some show remarkable resilience despite a history of abuse. The difference in vulnerability can often be traced to variant versions of a gene that controls a key brain enzyme, MAOA (monoamine oxidase A), which helps regulate the brain's response to stress.

A 2007 study, led by Italian researcher Francesca Ducci, found that women who carry a gene for low MAOA activity are strongly prone to becoming alcoholics if they were abused as children, while those with a high-activity MAOA gene, are much more resilient. It takes both the gene and the childhood trauma for the pattern to emerge. Among women who were not abused, there's no relationship between the MAOA gene and addiction.

Researchers hope that a better understanding of the genetics of addiction will lead to more effective treatments. Happily, that's already on the horizon.

The drug naltrexone was developed to treat alcoholism, but for many addicts, it's not terribly effective. Recent research

Genes and Environment

The idea that vulnerability to drug addiction can be inherited has been widely misunderstood. It is obvious—indeed it is a trivial statement—that if a drug were totally unavailable, no one could become addicted to it, regardless of their heredity. In that sense, drug addiction differs from clear-cut genetic diseases that do not depend on external factors. The position may be closer to that of diseases with strong hereditary influences like the common kinds of heart disease, or like cancers of the breast or colon, in which environmental factors play a major role.

The strong influence of environmental factors is nowhere more obvious than in nicotine addiction. Forty-five years ago, a large majority of young Americans began smoking as they entered adolescence, but today only a small minority (around one-fifth) become smokers. Moreover, of all the people who've ever smoked, two-thirds have been able to quit. Obviously the genes have not changed in 45 years; the change must be due to other factors such as intensive education about the health consequences of smoking. Unlike the genes, these other factors can be modified to reduce addictive behaviors—by prevention education and by laws restricting where and when smoking is allowed.

Avram Goldstein,
Addiction: From Biology to Drug Policy.
New York: Oxford University Press, 2001.

shows, however, that for a subset of alcoholics who have a genetic variation in one of their opioid receptors—25% to 30% of the population—the drug, which is used in conjunction with psychotherapy, works very well indeed.

University of Pennsylvania psychiatrist David Oslin and his colleagues are now conducting a trial to see if screening for this gene and prescribing the drug accordingly would lead to better outcomes in the notoriously difficult business of treating alcoholism.

Matching treatment to the patient's genotype could be the future of the field. And, Dr. Oslin observes, "It reinforces for the patients that they are not just a bad person or lack will-power. It resonates with the notion that their brain may work a little differently than other people's and that this really is an illness they can treat like any other."

Periodical and Internet Sources Bibliography

The following articles have been selected to supplement the diverse views presented in this chapter.

Carol Bennett — "The Road to Addiction—How Trauma Can Lead to Addiction," *Huffington Post*, August 1, 2009.

Benedict Carey — "In Clue to Addiction, Brain Injury Halts Smoking," *New York Times*, January 26, 2007.

Jennifer Chu — "The Genetics of Nicotine Addiction," *Technology Review*, March 8, 2007.

Alexis C. Edwards, Dace S. Svikis, Roy W. Pickens, and Danielle M. Dick — "Genetic Influences on Addiction," *Primary Psychiatry*, 2009.

Michael D. Lemonick — "How We Get Addicted," *Time*, July 5, 2007.

Ming D. Li and Margit Burmeister — "New Insights into the Genetics of Addiction," *Nature Reviews Genetics*, April 2009.

Stephen J. Morse — "Addiction, Genetics and Criminal Responsibility," *Law and Contemporary Problems*, vol. 69, 2006.

Sally Satel and Scott Lilienfeld — "Medical Misnomer," *Slate*, July 25, 2007.

ScienceDaily — "Addiction: A Loss of Plasticity of the Brain?" June 25, 2010.

Jennifer Thomas — "Marijuana, Alcohol Addiction May Share Genes," *U.S. News & World Report*, December 18, 2009.

Karen McNulty Walsh — "Brain-Behavior Disconnect in Cocaine Addiction," Medical News Today, May 26, 2009. www.medicalnewstoday.com.

 OPPOSING
VIEWPOINTS®
SERIES

What Drug Treatment and Prevention Programs Are Effective?

Chapter Preface

In March 2001 the US Supreme Court ruled that drug testing pregnant women without consent is unconstitutional. Furthermore, no state has specific laws that criminalize drug addiction for this group; prosecution is sought through drug distribution and child endangerment laws. The procedure, however, remains an ethical dilemma within health care settings. Proponents maintain that fetal alcohol syndrome is the leading preventable cause of birth defects and developmental disabilities in the nation, and screening is an invaluable tool to prevent harm to an unborn child. The Vermont Department of Health estimates that 10–15 percent of expectant mothers have a problem with substance abuse. "Since there are no defined safe limits during pregnancy, any use should be minimized,"[1] states department commissioner Wendy Davis. "Early identification is the first step toward engaging substance dependent women into treatment." The health department contends that every practice is responsible for screening all pregnant women and new mothers for alcohol, smoking, and other dependency issues.

Others disagree with the view that health care providers must drug test every pregnant woman, proposing that it could be an affront to the patient-physician relationship. "Health care professionals who act on behalf of the state rather than for their patients breach the ethical duties of the patient-physician relationship,"[2] argues Kristin Pulatie, a Chicago attorney. "Such a breach erodes confidence and trust in the medical community, resulting in poor disclosure by patients, which, in turn, may dramatically reduce the efficacy of diagnosis and treatment." Pulatie supports the Supreme Court de-

1. "Screening for Substance Abuse During Pregnancy: Guidelines for Screening," 2009.
2. *American Medical Association Journal of Ethics*, "The Legality of Drug-Testing Procedures for Pregnant Women," January 2008.

cision and says that it "recognizes that a physician's duty is to provide sound medical treatment to his patient, not to act as an extension of law enforcement." In the following chapter, the authors examine the effectiveness of various interventions of drug abuse and addiction.

"*Needle exchange is AIDS prevention that works.*"

Needle-Exchange Programs Can Reduce the Transmission of HIV

Tina Rosenberg

In the following viewpoint, Tina Rosenberg contends that intravenous drug use fuels HIV (human immunodeficiency virus) transmission rates: Addicts not only put themselves at risk when using unsterile needles but also risk exposing their sexual partners to the virus. Therefore, she insists that needle-exchange programs slow the spread of AIDS (acquired immune deficiency syndrome) while drawing addicts to counseling and rehabilitation services. Nonetheless, Rosenberg states that government support of such harm-reduction initiatives is lacking in the United States and abroad, especially in Russia, a country where HIV first spread intravenously. Rosenberg is a Pulitzer Prize–winning journalist and contributor to the New York Times Magazine.

Tina Rosenberg, "The Needle Nexus," *New York Times Magazine*, November 22, 2009. Reprinted by permission.

As you read, consider the following questions:

1. What figures does Rosenberg provide to bolster her claim that HIV is frequently spread through intravenous drug use?

2. As described by the author, what is the status of the federal government's support for needle exchange?

3. Why must governments support needle-exchange programs, in the author's view?

Of all the mysteries posed by AIDs [acquired immune deficiency syndrome], perhaps the deepest and most damaging is a human one: Why have we failed so utterly to stop its transmission? Most people with HIV [human immunodeficiency virus] in the world, including a vast majority of the 22 million who are infected in sub-Saharan Africa, caught it from a sexual partner. Despite billions of dollars spent to slow this form of transmission, only a few countries have had significant success—among them Thailand, Uganda and Zimbabwe—and their achievements have been unreplicable, poorly understood and short-lived. We know that abstinence, sexual fidelity and consistent condom use all prevent the spread of HIV. But we do not yet know how to persuade people to act accordingly.

Then there is another way that HIV infects: by injection with a hypodermic needle previously used by an infected person. Outside Africa, a huge part of the AIDS epidemic involves people who were infected this way. In Russia, 83 percent of infections in which the origin is known come from needle sharing. In Ukraine, the figure is 64 percent; Kazakhstan, 74 percent; Malaysia, 72 percent; Vietnam, 52 percent; China, 44 percent. Shared needles are also the primary transmission route for HIV in parts of Asia. In the United States, needle sharing directly accounts for more than 25 percent of AIDS cases.

Drug injectors don't pass infection only among themselves. Through their sex partners, HIV is spread into the general population. In many countries, the HIV epidemic began among drug injectors. In Russia in 2000, for example, needle sharing was directly responsible for more than 95 percent of all cases of HIV infection. So virtually all those with HIV in Russia can trace their infection to a shared needle not many generations back. Though it has been scorned as special treatment for a despised population, AIDS prevention for drug users is in fact crucial to preventing a wider epidemic.

Unlike with sexual transmission, there is a proven solution here: needle-exchange programs, which provide drug injectors with clean needles, usually in return for their used ones. Needle exchange is the cornerstone of an approach known as harm reduction, making drug use less deadly. Clean needles are both tool and lure, a way to introduce drug users to counseling, HIV tests, AIDS treatment and rehabilitation, including access to opioid-substitution therapies like methadone.

Trumped by Risky Politics

Needle exchange is AIDS prevention that works. While no one wants to have to put on a condom, every drug user prefers injuring with a clean needle. In 2003, an academic review of 99 cities around the world found that cities with needle exchange saw their HIV rates among injecting drug users drop 19 percent a year; cities without needle exchange had an 8 percent increase per year. Contrary to popular fears, needle exchange has not led to more drug use or higher crime rates. Studies have also found that drug addicts participating in needle exchanges are more likely to enter rehabilitation programs....

All over the world, however, solid evidence in support of needle exchange is trumped by its risky politics. Harm reduction is thought by politicians to muddy the message that drug use is bad; to have authorities handing out needles puts an official stamp of approval on dangerous behavior. Consider the United States. In 1988, Congress passed a ban on the use of federal money for needle exchange; President [Bill] Clinton said he supported needle exchange but never lifted the ban, and it remains in effect. It not only applies to programs inside the United States but also prohibits the U.S. Agency for International Development from financing needle-exchange programs in its AIDS prevention work anywhere in the world. The administration of George W. Bush made the policy more aggressive, pressuring United Nations [UN] agencies to retract their support for needle exchange and excise statements about its efficacy from their literature. (Today, UN agencies again recommend that needle exchange be part of HIV-prevention services for drug users.) Despite Barack Obama's campaign pledge to overturn the ban, his first budget retained it. The House of Representatives recently passed a bill that would lift the ban—but it includes a provision that would make using federal money for needle exchange virtually impossible in cities, where it is needed most.

There are some parts of the world—Western Europe, Australia, New Zealand—that do widely use harm-reduction strategies, including needle exchange. And programs have begun even in Iran, of all places, which offers needle exchange and methadone; its program of giving prisoners methadone is now the world's largest. China is now taking AIDS seriously, and is beginning to institute government-sponsored harm reduction nationwide. But the overwhelming majority of drug injectors around the world still have no such access. Because government financing is so politically unpopular, in most of the 77 countries that offer needle exchange, the programs are run by nongovernmental groups. As a result, these efforts are small, isolated and often undermined by uncooperative police and health departments. The world is casting aside the single most effective AIDS prevention strategy we know.

A Guerilla Effort

Russia needs needle exchange more than any other country: Its HIV epidemic is large, one of the fastest-growing in the world, and perhaps the most dominated by injecting drug use. Yet the needle-exchange efforts that do exist are scarce, small and under siege. I traveled there recently to see what lessons they hold. At 9 p.m. on a May night, in a tough neighborhood in Moscow's north, I joined two young men as they climbed the stairs from the Metro. Arseniy and David were in their late 20s, wearing jeans and baseball caps. They had arrived to give out clean needles and promote harm reduction—but theirs was a guerrilla effort.

Needle exchange is legal in Russia—sort of. It must follow federal regulations. The catch is that these regulations don't exist: the Federal Drug Control Service, whose top officials have called needle exchange "nothing more than open propaganda for drugs," has been sitting on them for five years. As a result, no new harm-reduction programs have started during that time. Old ones continue where local authorities tolerate them, but Moscow's government disapproves of needle exchange. So like their clients, Arseniy and David avoid the police. One of their clients was Masha, who, like every other drug user I interviewed, talked about police extortion. It is every addict's main fear, but avoiding police shakedowns means only more dangerous injecting: If you fear being caught walking around with a needle, you use the community needle your dealer provides.

Arseniy told me that he started doing harm reduction as a volunteer with an organization working with the homeless. "Most of my clients used drugs, and I understood we couldn't do anything without needle exchange," he said. So the workers began buying needles with their own money and giving them out. Now he, David and another pair of outreach workers get financing from another Russian group. The city of Moscow, then, has only a handful of people doing needle exchange. An extremely conservative estimate of Moscow's drug injectors puts the number at 240,000.

Moscow's drug policy could be called harm augmentation; discourage drug use by making it as dangerous as possible. Arseniy and David for example, can't direct addicts to methadone clinics, since methadone—the global gold standard rehabilitation method—is illegal in Russia. Nor can they bring users into the health system: Beyond the most basic health services, public health care in Moscow is only for officially registered residents; many drug injectors are homeless or from other cities and are unregistered in Moscow. The only thing Arseniy and David can do is give out the card of a drop-in center, called Yasen, across the city from the clients they were serving.

When I visited Yasen, staff members told me stories of ambulances refusing to pick up an overdosing drug user and hospitals turning away people who come in with the afflictions of a violent life on the streets. Russia does have free detoxification clinics, but they use harsh, outdated methods, and less than 10 percent of their clients stay drug free for a year. Checking in lands an addict on the official list of drug users—a designation that can affect opportunities for jobs, housing and privileges like driver's licenses.

A Model Program

While the city of Moscow treats drug users purely as potential criminals, St. Petersburg is different. The main reason is the work of Humanitarian Action, among Russia's first needle-exchange programs, which started its work in 1997. The heart of Humanitarian Action is its mobile clinic, a blue bus that visits 10 neighborhoods a week on a regular schedule. On a Friday afternoon when I visited, the bus was parked on the side of a busy street in front of a block of apartment towers. There was a line out the back door of people returning bags of used needles and getting clean ones.

A Tough Sell

The controversy over needle-exchange programs designed to provide drug users with sterile injecting equipment has simmered for almost a decade. Despite shockingly high rates of infection among IDUs [intravenous drug users] and increasing scientific evidence supporting the efficacy of needle exchange, Congress has repeatedly gone out of its way to prohibit the federal funding of needle exchange. Explaining this puzzle requires understanding the complexities of politics in the United States and appreciating the bind that elected lawmakers find themselves in when they make policies that single out citizens, in this case the highly unpopular population of "drug users." These quotes highlight the rhetorical dimension of politics, the ways that political language and political communication influence policy making. Although many needle-exchange proponents bemoan the triumph of "politics" over "science," such a formulation ignores an array of factors that makes needle exchange a tough sell.

William N. Elwood, ed.,
Power in the Blood: A Handbook on
AIDS, Politics, and Communication.
Mahwah, NJ: Lawrence Erlbaum Associates Inc., 1999.

Lena Porechenkova, a skinny, grizzled woman with tinted glasses, was running the bus's needle-exchange counter. She spoke to a fresh-faced woman of 22, also named Lena. She was planning to quit, Lena said. "But I don't want to get onto the state list of addicts and have problems getting a job later." She said she might consider buying methadone (often sold illegally by heroin dealers) and trying to quit on her own.

"Well, it's possible to overcome this on your own," Porechenkova said, but she added that it is possible to pay $200 and be anonymous. "Why don't you talk to our psychologist?" She called over Nikolai Yekimov, who took Lena into a tiny office in the bus. Yekimov has a database of rehabilitation centers. The bus also offers a case manager, who helps the client assemble the necessary papers and test results and will even pick her up and accompany her to the clinic. When Lena left, I asked her where she would go for advice if the bus didn't exist. "Nowhere," she said.

Humanitarian Action is a model program. It has everything harm reduction needs—save the most important thing: size. The group estimates that it has 4,000 repeat clients—a tiny proportion of St. Petersburg's drug injectors, who number as many as 150,000.

In a few Russian cities needle-exchange programs run by the municipal or regional governments have kept HIV rates among drug users relatively low. But most of the country's 75 harm-reduction programs—almost all of which do needle exchange—are run by Russian nongovernmental groups with money from the Global Fund to Fight AIDS, Tuberculosis and Malaria. These programs run on $20,000 to $30,000 a year, which is far too small to have an impact. And they are imperiled. Russia is now too rich to accept Global Fund grants for HIV prevention, so these programs will lose their financing over the next two years. Russian officials are resisting requests from international AIDS advocates to keep needle exchange alive.

The future of harm reduction does not reside in small programs carried out by internationally financed groups, however stellar their quality. Such programs have proved that harm reduction works, but they cannot make it epidemiologically relevant. Only a government can ensure that the police and hospitals will respect drug users' rights to health care. Only a government can do needle exchange on a wide scale. This is what is needed to reduce HIV rates—not just for drug users, but for us all.

"There is no guarantee how the new needle is used once the addict departs with it."

Needle-Exchange Programs May Not Reduce the Transmission of HIV

Robert John Araujo

In the following viewpoint, Robert John Araujo states that needle-exchange programs do not safeguard intravenous drug users from blood-borne diseases. Ensuring that addicts use clean or new needles each time is impossible and defeats the goal of reducing HIV (human immunodeficiency virus) transmissions, Araujo argues. Additionally, he disagrees with the principle that addiction is a lesser evil than HIV and AIDS (acquired immune deficiency syndrome). Araujo writes that substance abuse is just as destructive to health and a source of suffering; therefore, treatment and rehabilitation should replace needle-exchange programs. The author is a professor at Loyola University's School of Law in Chicago, Illinois, and a Roman Catholic friar.

Robert John Araujo, "Thoughts on the Needle Exchange Program Adopted by the Diocese of Albany," Mirror of Justice Blog, February 10, 2010. Reprinted by permission.

As you read, consider the following questions:

1. In Araujo's opinion, what are the alternatives to needle-exchange programs?

2. What is Araujo's view of the claim that needle-exchange programs lead to treatment and recovery?

3. How does Araujo respond to the assertion that studies validate the effectiveness of needle exchange in saving lives?

I should like to thank [Cornell Law School faculty member] Bob Hockett for his bringing to our attention the *Washington Post* article published earlier today [February 13, 2010] on the Albany Diocese's needle-exchange program. In short, the thrust of the argument appears to be: It is a choice between the lesser of two evils. Is it really? Is there any guarantee that once the addict leaves the distribution center or centers administered by the diocese he or she will use it once and then return it prior to the time the next "fix" is required? It is apparent that there will be no supervision by [Project] Safe Point in how the new needle is used and for how long by the addict of illegal drugs. Moreover, there appears to be no recognition that at some point, all hypodermic syringes are new—even the used one being returned for an exchange was new at one time. . . .

No Lesser Evil

First of all, let us consider the contention that, while illegal drug use is bad, the spread of deadly disease is worse. Let us test the soundness of this proposition. I begin with the distinction that this statement makes that blood-borne diseases are deemed a greater evil than drug addiction and the addictions' essential surrounding issues. It is false. Illegal drug use is no lesser an evil because without appropriate medical treatment, the spiral of the addict will progress downward until the day that the addict's body can no longer sustain the chemical abuse, and he or she dies from an overdose or other complications. There is no good ending to untreated drug abuse with serious and illegal drugs that require injection by hypodermic syringes. The addict is constantly hanging over a pit of destruction started by himself or herself and then sustained . . . by drug lords who have little interest in anything but more profit. By providing a needle-exchange program, any institution is at a minimum turning a blind eye to the profit-driven motivations that prey on human life without mercy and the destruction of life that this chemical dependency generates. Are there alternatives? Of course there are. Treatment programs, job counseling programs, and other projects that could be substituted for needle-exchange programs help the addict far more than assistance that will only sustain the addict's dependency but do nothing about it. By providing a needle-exchange program, the addict's life remains over the pit of destruction without any hope of rescue other than trying to reduce infections from blood-borne diseases. But as I have already mentioned, there is no guarantee how the new needle is used once the addict departs with it. How "public health authorities" referred to by the *Post* article can assert that needle-exchange programs can "even lead drug abusers to treatment and recovery" makes no appeal based on reason. If the destructive habit is being sustained by "well-intentioned programs," how can the addict turn to the path of treatment and recovery? The craving that is an inevitable part of drug dependency will not vanish with new needles. I fail to see the logic in the arguments offered by the proponents of needle exchange as presented and only recognize an unsupportable claim. The addict remains enslaved to a self-destructive habit, which robs him or her of human dignity and life. There is no charity or solidarity or mercy extended to this victim of chemical dependency, only abandonment is offered so that the dependency increases while the drug lords grow richer. Somehow this fact, which ought to be inescapable, escapes those who support needle-exchange programs.

The diocese then asserts that the "Safe Point" program "is based upon the Church's [sic] standard moral principles." In theory, it may be possible to argue in the proper contexts "double effect" or "choosing the lesser of two evils" or, for some moralists, "proportionalism" or "consequentialism." But these justifications do not apply here. [The latter two, i.e., proportionalism and consequentialism, are plagued with their own problems, which I won't go into today since they have not been raised by any of the moralists quoted in the *Post* article.] Why? I suggest these elements of "the Church's [sic] standard moral principles" cannot overlook the spectrum of the constitutive elements of both evils, i.e., drug addiction and infectious disease that is generated by drug abuse. In the final analysis, they are both evil in their own right, and it would be unsound to suggest that one is less problematic than the other. While they may intersect the life of the same person, one is not disproportionate to the other.

In the preparation of its article, the *Post* consulted with a variety of individuals in demonstrating the spectrum of views that favor and that object to needle-exchange programs administered by the Church's corporal works of mercy. I begin with the remarks attributed to Dr. Edward Peters, who is both a canonist and a civil law lawyer. He has addressed the Albany Diocese exchange program at his own website, and I believe his in-depth reflections need to be studied carefully because he is on to something vital regarding these issues and the debate surrounding them.

No Guarantee

The *Post* then turns to three priests, yes, all are Jesuits, and yes, I am familiar with them and their work. My comments in no way reflect a lack of fraternal concern of or respect for them; however, on the issue of supporting needle-exchange programs by relying on their versions of Catholic moral principles, I must state my disagreement and explain why. Unfortunately for Fr. [James] Bretzke, a professor of moral theology at Boston College, the *Post* merely states that by relying on the "lesser evil" argument, the Diocese of Albany is relying, in part, on a Thomistic [philosophy of St. Thomas Aquinas] principle. But as I have stated earlier, the issues involved here are much more involved than giving "safe" needles versus risking infection from blood-borne diseases and assuming that one evil is lesser than the other. Let us understand the distinction clearly: The rational agent must conclude that he or she is not simply giving an addict a clean needle so that the addict will be free from a contaminated needle. As already stated, there is no guarantee that the new needle will be used only once and only by the addict to whom it is given. No one, including the addict, can predict if this needle will not be used again by the addict or anyone else. The hope that this will not happen is misplaced. In addition, the purported "lesser evil" is a complex one with many tentacles that ensnare the unwary and the unthinking. There is no promise of treatment and cure with a needle-exchange program without something more being offered to assist the addict; the inexorable potential is that the chemical dependency without further intervention will therefore be sustained indefinitely. The other thing that will be sustained is the boldness of the dealers whose desire it is to keep the addict addicted. And with their business uninterrupted, will they not look for new markets to sell their poison? These are surely elements of the "Safe Point" program that lurk in the side wings but have not been addressed by the needle-exchange proponents. Fr. Bretzke further states if: "you cannot reasonably expect a person to avoid the moral evil itself [i.e., illegal drug use], you can counsel them or mitigate the potential damage of their action and can even help them in doing that." If the concern he expresses is only mitigation through needle exchange, his conclusion is wrong. If the needle-exchange program were substituted with counseling and medical treatment that assists the addict in overcoming the chemical dependency, then yes, Fr. Bretzke would be on the correct track because the addict would then be given assistance to overcome the moral evil of illegal drug dependency.

Wishful Thinking

The aspiration that "Safe Point" will decrease or eliminate infections of blood-borne diseases by the addict who exchanges the needle or by other addicts is wishful thinking but little else. Blood-borne diseases of any kind are an enormous problem, and deaths caused by such diseases are avoidable. Dependency on illegal, potent drugs is also an enormous problem, and it, too, causes deaths. So, is death by drug dependency or death by blood-borne diseases any different? No. But can we as a society and Church that cares about people through our exercise of Christian charity avoid both? To borrow from a high-level public official, "yes, we can!" And we can do so if we recognize that both are evils that can be avoided and, at the same time, acknowledge that one is not the lesser evil than the other.

Rev. [Jon] Fuller, a well-known Boston physician, is quoted as saying, "If we know programs are scientifically validated to save lives, then condemning them can be more scandalous than the possibility of being seen to condone drug use." I suggest that this "if" is a pretty big one. Let us be clear about the distinction he makes: Does the program that is "scientifically validated" ensure that no needle from a needle-exchange program is ever used more than once? He does not mention this. I wonder if there is an assumption that no needle is used more than once. It may be that the needle is used by the exchanging addict only once, but does the "scientifically validated" program take stock of the possibility, perhaps probability, that someone else may use the needle, since it is "almost new," before it is exchanged? I wonder. Fr. Fuller does speak about a possibility elsewhere, but it is only in the context that there is a possibility that needle-exchange programs may condone the use of drug use. No, the scandal is more than "possibly condoning drug use." The scandal is that it, at a minimum, constitutes material cooperation with a distinct, but not lesser evil. I am prepared ... to demonstrate that a needle-exchange program is, in fact, formal cooperation with evil that can be and must be avoided. A needle-exchange program's officials cannot overlook the fact that drug addicts are destroying their lives while drug dealers and distributors and manufacturers of controlled substances increase their profits and are then encouraged to look for new markets. To provide needles in an exchange program and overlook these undeniable realities of drug addiction is a scandal of enormous magnitude that is independent of scandals of denying addicts clean needles in the hope of avoiding life-threatening blood-borne illnesses.

The *Post* also quotes Fr. James Keenan, also another professor of moral theology at Boston College. The article mentions that he "successfully pushed ... a nondenominational association of scholars, to pass a resolution in support of needle-exchange programs." I wonder what the resolution states and the reasoning used to justify it? Did those voting in favor of it consider the points I have addressed demonstrating the problems inherent in the justifications given for the Albany Diocese's program? I agree with Fr. Keenan that the Church and her corporal works of mercy must be about love of neighbor, the common good, human dignity, and responding to human suffering. But, as I have demonstrated, mercy, love of neighbor, the common good, human dignity, and responding to human suffering are not well served when problems are intensified rather than remedied for those addicts whom the Church is attempting to help. I must unfortunately disagree with Fr. Keenan's assertion that the Albany Catholic

Charities "just gave us the answer." They gave no answer but have, I believe, made a serious problem worse for the intravenous illegal drug user.

Not Something to Celebrate

Let me conclude this lengthy posting with a reference to Dr. Germain Grisez's discussion in the *Post* article. There is far more involved with needle exchanges than just needle exchanges. I hope to have demonstrated that. Dr. Grisez states that the Church has a caretaker role in the betterment of the human person and should not be involved in needle-exchange programs. By way of illustrating my point, let us say that the Albany Diocese was not involved in a needle-exchange program but a project designed to help alcoholics. If the diocese's Catholic Charities offered counseling and medical treatment for the alcoholics, I think most would agree that this would be a meritorious project supported by the Church's moral teachings and social doctrine. But what if, instead, the diocese took a different track and set up cocktail lounges that catered to alcoholics and operated under the project name "Safe Point." What would be the reaction then? You would be correct in labeling this project indefensible. So, too, is the needle-exchange program.

"Safe Point" is not something to celebrate. It is not something to promote. It is not something to rationalize as the lesser of two evils. It is, ultimately, something to lament because of what it is and what it does to human life. Complicating the lament that makes it a tragedy is the fact that the Diocese of Albany, through its Catholic Charities, had and still has alternatives that do not require the cooperation—formal or material—with drug dependency. Sadly, and for the time being, the diocese has not chosen the better and moral path. Let us pray that it will be corrected, and soon because human life, human dignity, the common good, and alleviating human suffering remain at risk.

> "Originally greeted with skepticism and suspicion, methadone has survived to become an established treatment for heroin abuse."

Methadone Is an Effective Treatment for Heroin Addiction

Ira J. Marion

Based in New York City, Ira J. Marion is executive director of the Division of Substance Abuse at Yeshiva University's Albert Einstein College of Medicine. In the following viewpoint, Marion endorses the efficacy and safety of methadone treatment for opiate addiction. After decades of research and clinical experience, he states that today's drug abuse specialists have the tools, knowledge, and skills to respond to the physical, mental, and social needs of patients. Through adequate methadone dosing, attention to other conditions, and flexible treatment arrangements, the objectives to suppress cravings and improve overall health are being met, Marion says.

Ira J. Marion, "Methadone Treatment at Forty," *Science & Practice Perspectives*, vol. 3, no. 1, December 2005, p. 25–32. Reprinted by permission.

As you read, consider the following questions:

1. As stated by Marion, what are the intermediate goals of methadone treatment?

2. What research does Marion cite to support his assertion that methadone is key in ending opiate addiction?

3. What recommendation does the author have in educating the public of methadone and heroin abuse?

As methadone maintenance treatment enters its fifth decade, opioid treatment programs (OTPs) are drawing on lessons learned from past successes and failures to continuously improve the treatment modality. Today's patients span an age range wider than ever before, and present with a greater quantity and severity of addictions and health problems. In the face of this, OTPs have access to improved research and technology, and have also developed a greater understanding of the full dimensions of opioid addiction and recovery. We now know that opioid addiction is a chronic disease, so we no longer think of methadone as a short-term bridge to recovery, but instead consider it an intervention that may be beneficial indefinitely. . . .

Treatment Goals and Features

The defining characteristic of care in today's OTPs, distinguishing them from those in the past, is increased tailoring of treatment to each patient's individual goals and needs. Four decades of clinical experience and research have equipped OTP clinicians with awareness, tools, and skills to adapt care plans to a wide range of physical and mental health comorbidities, family and social circumstances, and recovery expectations.

Treatment Goals. The initial technical goals of methadone treatment are to relieve the patient's narcotic craving, suppress the abstinence syndrome, and block the euphoric effects associated with heroin. The overall goal is to improve the patient's health and quality of life. Intermediate objectives include improving patients' access to and utilization of health care, teaching them to reduce their risk for infectious diseases such as HIV (human immunodeficiency virus) and hepatitis, and helping them build healthy relationships and re-enter the workforce or school.

The cumulative experience with methadone has led providers to re-examine one of the original assumptions regarding this therapy: that all patients should strive to be drug free. In recent years, a gathering consensus has endorsed methadone maintenance as a chronic, potentially lifelong treatment. This view harmonizes with recent emphasis on the chronic, episodic nature of heroin addiction.

The public and policy makers are making this conceptual adjustment more slowly, which can lead to some tension over expectations. Many patients, particularly in their first treatment episode, want to taper their methadone dosage when their cravings subside and they see themselves progressing in other areas of their lives. Although some truly can abstain from methadone and still have reasonable hope for stable long-term recovery, overall, research has found that up to 80 percent of patients who quit methadone relapse to opioid abuse within 3 years. In our program, we teach that the measure of success is not whether you take a medicine in the morning, but whether you take care of yourself and your family, act responsibly, and contribute to society. Even those who can thrive without methadone are unlikely to do so unless they remain connected to some form of treatment.

Dose and Schedule

Methadone dosing is a prime area where the principle of individualized treatment has emerged in sharp contrast to past practice. Clinicians today benefit from developments that have greatly enhanced the ability to identify and provide each patient with a dosage that completely suppresses craving and heroin abuse and produces minimal side effects.

First, we have learned that adequate dosage varies greatly. While some individuals do well on as little as 20 mg/day, others require up to 10 or 15 times as much or more. Differences in native metabolism and in the effects of methadone's interaction with other concurrent medications underlie this wide range. The most frequently encountered interactions occur in patients receiving medications for HIV—some of which speed and some of which slow methadone metabolism—and for hepatitis C. Patients taking interferon for hepatitis C may need upward adjustment in their methadone dosage to counteract a toxic effect of the antiviral medication that mimics opioid withdrawal.

The patient's response to methadone—whether he or she continues to crave or abuse heroin, or feels excessively drowsy—is the essential indicator of whether the prescribed dosage is too little or too much. To determine this, we talk with the patient to find out if he or she has tried taking opioids while on methadone, and, if so, why and what kind of opioid effect was felt. We ask what time of day drug-taking occurs, which is oftentimes when methadone blood levels are bottoming out.

The move to fully individualized dosing, like the acceptance of indefinitely long methadone therapy, has not yet happened everywhere. A few states still place ceilings on prescription amounts. A recent study of about 30 OTPs over a 10-year period found that programs where doctors freely determined methadone dosage were more likely to give adequate amounts than programs where public policy limited the options.

Attention to Co-Occurring Conditions. Today's OTPs recognize the adverse impact of co-occurring addictions and comorbid illnesses on their patients' progress in treatment, but, in general, we have yet to evolve broadly applicable standards for responding. Given their very long-term trend toward ever-higher prevalence, these problems are prime candidates for research attention. Unfortunately, even where research has proven one or another approach to be effective, funding limitations prohibit many programs from implementing the best practices.

Co-Occurring Addictions. Some OTPs insist that patients attend groups and honestly address their co-occurring addictions in treatment or else face termination; others do not place limits on treatment and continue to try to motivate patients to stop using non-opioid drugs. Studies have shown that medications can help patients in methadone treatment reduce alcohol and cocaine abuse (amantadine, serotonin reuptake inhibitors). In one study, investigators used a breathalyzer test to determine which patients were the worst abusers of alcohol, then asked these patients to either begin taking Antabuse or transfer to another clinic. All agreed to take Antabuse and, for the length of the 90-day study, none drank alcohol.

Whatever a program's policies may be, clinicians need to consider each patient's overall behavior when deciding how to react to his or her abuse of other drugs. A patient who is honest about drug abuse and wants to stop should not be treated in the same manner as one who refuses to attend group meetings or follow through with treatment plans or activities. The former is struggling with craving and making an effort; the latter does not appear motivated to accept treatment.

Co-Occurring Medical Illnesses. Methadone programs that offer comprehensive mental and physical health services obtain significantly better outcomes for their patients. One particularly successful model is "one-stop shopping," where patients receive all services at the same site. While these principles are well accepted across the field, many smaller programs lack the resources to put them into practice. These programs instead refer patients to other facilities, encourage them to follow up, and hope they do. The hopeful element in today's picture, discussed below, is that mainstream medical practitioners increasingly are willing to treat drug-abusing patients.

Treatment Delivery Systems. Today's OTPs have begun to evolve past the original, rigid treatment delivery system that requires every patient to report to a clinic for each day's methadone dose. In New York and some other locations, clinics are implementing flexible, tiered systems that respond to patients' personal growth and changing circumstances as they advance in recovery.

Medical maintenance, a promising new arrangement, allows individuals who have passed the initial phases of therapy to obtain treatment in a physician's office. At New York[-Presbyterian] Hospital/[Weill] Cornell Medical [College] in New York City, for example, the patient sees a doctor once a month, leaves a specimen for drug testing, and gets a methadone prescription to fill at a local pharmacy. He or she does not have to choose between tapering and permanent clinic attendance, with its potentially demoralizing exposure to the milieu of recent heroin abuse. The arrangement recognizes that these individuals have achieved significant control over their illness, helps them establish normal physician-patient relationships, and enables them to schedule treatment that doesn't conflict with jobs or other social obligations. As well, our office-based opioid treatment frees up clinic beds for new patients who require more structured services.

Another new model, the treatment phase approach, divides treatment into highly structured stages. All patients participate in the first three: intensive stabilization, commitment, and rehabilitation. Patients then choose, with the help of their doctors, between two tracks: medical maintenance or tapering. The final phase is reinforcement. OTPs using the treatment phase model front-load their services to the people entering treatment, who have the most need, involving them in good health care, educating them about HIV and hepatitis C, and

Inherently Evil

The public misplaces a moral quality to drugs. Narcotics, which include methadone, are perceived as inherently evil. A philosophical orientation is placed within structure of heroin and methadone and the social stigma is therefore not only transferred to individuals but to the medications they are taking to control their addiction. Methadone itself becomes stigmatized. The political and social roles of drugs and medications influence the perception of the pharmacology.

Joycelyn Sue Woods,
"The Penal Attitude and Methadone Treatment,"
Journal of Maintenance in the Addictions, *January 1997.*

introducing them to outside resources that will provide the medical care and social services they need. The clinic staff works with patients to formulate treatment plans that address patients' problems in order of urgency, such as criminal justice, mental illness, housing, employment, and education. As the first set of problems ease, the staff implements new services for the next most serious until, eventually, the cumulative improvement eliminates the need for most services.

A Mainstream Medical Treatment

Originally greeted with skepticism and suspicion, methadone has survived to become an established treatment for heroin abuse. Although negative perceptions and stigma still persist in an attenuated form—and everyone looks forward to the day when OTPs can produce long-term recovery more quickly and consistently—by and large, heroin abusers, communities, policy makers, and researchers now accept that the therapy's proven efficacy makes it worth trying, supporting, and refining. In this new climate of increased tolerance, methadone therapy has entered a transition from the margin toward the mainstream of medicine.

The Partial Retreat of Stigma

The disclosure through scientific research that addiction is a chronic disease, bolstered by examples of successful recovery, has tempered the stigmatizing of methadone patients and their treatment. The shift toward a health-based rather than moral concept of addiction, while not yet complete, has progressed remarkably swiftly, when we consider that it was only in 1997 that the National Institutes of Health first urged this view on the medical establishment.

Despite this greater tolerance of opioid replacement treatment, methadone diversion and loitering near clinics remain potent sources of negative attitudes toward OTPs. Neighbors tend to notice those individuals who hang around, get arrested, and require ambulance transport to the emergency room, rather than the majority who simply walk in and out of the clinic and get on with their lives. Taxpayers are loath to see their money going to provide addicted individuals with opioids to sell to other drug-abusing individuals. As well, although an investigation determined that diversion from OTPs has not been the primary cause of a recent increase in methadone-related death rates, communities fear the medication's potential lethality.

Strengthening communication between OTPs and their communities and stakeholders has proved an effective strategy for allaying these legitimate but exaggerated concerns. Many programs now attend planning board, precinct council, and other meetings where they can hear and respond to community worries or complaints. As OTPs have become more integrated into their communities over the decades, we have found natural allies in churches, synagogues, mosques, and even police departments and child welfare agencies. All share the mission of assisting the underserved, and all seek to strengthen messages of sense and tolerance.

Some regulatory authorities now provide their own impetus for OTPs to take active steps to improve the public's perceptions. New York State, for example, requires programs to solicit and address community concerns and criticisms. Center for Substance Abuse Treatment (CSAT) and accreditation regulations require programs to implement plans to control methadone dose diversion. The programs must know where their patients go after they leave the clinic and also assess their patients for potential diversion.

Physician Engagement. Physician investment in methadone therapy stands at its highest level ever. In the early days, some programs were lucky if they could find a part-time or retired physician to come in and oversee the methadone prescribing. Now, we turn away highly trained doctors.

Many doctors first became interested in methadone in the late 1980s, when studies showed that patients in treatment had lower rates of HIV infection than active heroin injectors. These doctors initially approached methadone therapy primarily as a way to slow the AIDS (acquired immune deficiency syndrome) epidemic through testing, educating, and counseling intravenous drug abusers. Subsequently, through involvement with the patients and programs, many have become fully engaged in the issues of addiction itself. . . .

Wish List

As OTPs continue to progress toward outcome-based treatment standards and integration with mainstream medicine, we can anticipate growing success in helping our patients meet the many challenges of their addictions and their lives. The continuation of these trends, together with further increases in the public and professional acceptance of methadone, must be at the top of everyone's wish list for methadone treatment. Beyond that, I believe the following developments could advance the cause dramatically:

- A medication for cocaine addiction.

- Upgrading of the physical facilities and locations of clinics. The current placement of most facilities in cramped spaces in shabby buildings in marginal neighborhoods can make the treatment experience awkward and intimidating. Ideally, clinics should have the physical space to allow staff to give private, confidential treatment, while also having larger areas for group meetings.

- More effective standardized assessment tools for patients with serious comorbidities, such as polysubstance abuse and mental illness. The Addiction Severity Index and other existing tools are useful, but we need a set of standardized tools that are specifically for methadone treatment, and that all our clinicians, with their array of educational backgrounds, can use to guide the treatment planning process.

- A concerted effort to educate the public on the benefits of methadone treatment. A federal effort to reduce the stigma associated with methadone treatment could help educate people on the nature of drug addictions and on why methadone is so important, not only to those who abuse drugs, but to society as a whole.

| "*Methadone is especially dangerous in unskilled hands.*"

Methadone Can Be Dangerous

JoNel Aleccia

In the following viewpoint, JoNel Aleccia suggests that methadone can be deadly in the wrong hands, noting that it has resulted in more fatalities than heroin in Spokane, Washington, in recent years. The long half-life of the substance—how long it remains in the human body—has led individuals who do not understand how methadone works to unintentionally overdose, the author adds. Likewise, she writes that the low street price and availability of its prescriptions dangerously place methadone out of medical and supervised usage. Aleccia reports on health for MSNBC.com and is a former staff writer for the Spokesman-Review *in Spokane, Washington.*

As you read, consider the following questions:

1. What figures does the author provide to back her statement that methadone killed more people than heroin, cocaine, and methamphetamine in Spokane during 2006?

JoNel Aleccia, "One Father's War on Methadone," *Spokesman-Review*, June 24, 2007. Reproduced by permission.

2. According to Aleccia, how do youths most commonly obtain methadone?

3. As stated in the viewpoint, what is the profile of a methadone abuser?

Standing in the dim basement where a methadone overdose killed his son, Ken Zigler prepared to honor Tim's legacy the only way he knows how.

The 52-year-old Spokane remodeling contractor squared his shoulders, set his jaw and swallowed hard before explaining, yet again, how the common prescription drug is ending more lives than any illicit substance.

"There's a lot of people that still don't have a clue," said Zigler.

Until March 27, 2006, Zigler didn't know much about the powerful painkiller, either. That changed the morning he found 17-year-old Tim barely breathing after ingesting what Zigler believes was 10 milligrams of methadone the night before.

"His lips were blue, he was unconscious," recalls Zigler. "I thought, 'Oh, no.'"

By the time paramedics arrived Zigler's youngest boy was gone.

Channeling Grief into Action

In the months since then, Zigler has channeled grief into action, becoming a one-man resource on the growing danger of the drug that continues to fuel a rise in overdose deaths in Spokane County.

He speaks to groups of parents and treatment professionals. He packs his truck with bumper stickers and windshield fliers that read: "Methadone is killing innocent Americans." He talks, again and again, to any young person willing to listen.

It helps Zigler stay connected to the quiet, dark-eyed young man who should have graduated this month [June 2007] from Ferris High School. And it helps him have hope for the future.

"Every day I'll contact somebody," Zigler said. "It's the only way I can justify Tim's death. It's the only thing that makes sense. Otherwise, it was for nothing."

In 2006, the year Tim died, methadone accounted for more deaths than cocaine, methamphetamine and heroin combined, according to records from the Spokane County Medical Examiner's Office.

Of the 112 people who died from accidental or intentional overdoses in 2006, nearly half—51—succumbed to methadone, either alone or in combination with other drugs.

By contrast, records show that cocaine and methamphetamine killed 36 people and heroin just one.

Actual incidents may not be quite as precise as they appear because of the way drugs and deaths are logged, said Dr. Sally Aiken, the medical examiner. But there's no doubt that deaths from prescription medication overdoses are far outpacing deaths from illicit drugs.

"It's not declining," Aiken said.

Although the average age of victims was 41, the drugs did not discriminate. Victims included boys as young as 16, women and men as old as 70, and people of all ages in between—including many who simply didn't realize that a substance that came from a medicine cabinet could be so dangerous.

"It's one of the medications where the difference between what works and what kills you isn't that different," Aiken said. "Just taking a little too much is significant."

Methadone Use Is on the Rise

Overall, the number of drug deaths was up slightly from 2005, when 103 people died of accidental or intentional overdoses and methadone was the primary culprit, according to a report expected to be posted this week on the medical examiner's Web site.

It's a trend that's not new to Spokane drug treatment providers like Tracy Varner, clinical director of Daybreak Drug and Alcohol Treatment.

"We've seen a huge shift in prescription drug use in the past two years," said Varner, whose agency provides inpatient and outpatient services to 1,100 young people annually. "There's a huge market in Spokane."

Unlike illicit drugs like methamphetamine, cocaine and heroin, methadone and other opiates are easily accessible and fairly cheap—about $60 to $70 for an 80-milligram pill.

"They can chop that bad boy up," Varner said. "That'll keep them high for days."

Getting the drugs is no problem, even for the 12-year-old Varner admitted to her program last week. Younger users take pills from their parents' medicine cabinets. Older kids buy them from sources who benefit from what some say are lax habits among doctors who over-prescribe painkillers, sometimes out of ignorance, sometimes intentionally.

"The biggest problem in this community is the diversion," said Aiken. "It's not being used by the person it's prescribed for."

And it's not being used by people who fit any expected profile for drug abuse, she added. Users span income, occupation and geography, often showing up in rural areas rather than urban centers. Utah, for instance, is reporting a growing prescription overdose problem, Aiken noted.

"The people that are dying from methadone aren't hardcore drug users," she said. "In our society, people think prescription medications are OK."

While all prescription drugs should be taken as directed, methadone is especially dangerous in unskilled hands. Unlike

Enough to Kill

Unfortunately, methadone is a very dangerous drug. Five milliliters [ml]—a teaspoonful—is enough to kill a baby, and 40ml is enough to kill an adult who is not habituated to opiates. The dangers are not merely theoretical . . . from time to time one reads in the medical press of doctors who have been struck off the medical register for negligently believing the lies their patients tell them about the amount of methadone they take, amounts that promptly kill their patients.

Theodore Dalrymple,
"An Official License to Kill,"
New Statesman, *March 3, 2003.*

some opiates, it takes longer to have an effect, and it accumulates in the system with what experts call a longer "half-life."

That means people hoping to relieve pain or achieve a high may take more and more of the drug because they don't see an immediate reaction. By the time it takes full effect, it may be too late. Methadone kills primarily by slowing respiration, overriding the body's instinct to breathe.

The trouble, said Varner, is that too few users recognize the danger.

"A lot of people who use drugs don't know about half-life," she said.

A Painful History

Tim Zigler had his share of struggles, his father said. The boy lost his mother to cancer when he was 4 and grew up close to his dad. Two years ago, Ken Zigler married his former sister-in-law, Stephanie, who had known Tim since he was a baby.

Tim was a quiet kid and an even quieter young man who got steady, if not sterling, grades and favored shop classes in school. He worked hard at his job in the housekeeping department at Spokane Valley Mall, mostly to afford payments on the green Honda Civic that was his pride.

Ken Zigler said his son, like many teens, smoked marijuana and experimented with alcohol. But he didn't use more potent drugs, his father said. That's why he was so sensitive to the low dose of methadone he ingested before he died. The fatal drug came, Zigler said, from a pretty and persistent girl Tim Zigler met at high school. Stephanie C. Davis was 16 when she was charged with homicide by drug abuse in Spokane County juvenile court in May 2006.

The girl was mandated to drug court last fall, with the understanding that if she failed to stay off drugs, graduate from high school and meet other requirements, she would face a bench trial based on her confessions to police. In January, she was sentenced to five days detention for testing positive for marijuana and not showing up for required drug tests.

A few months after the court hearing, Zigler said he saw the girl in the middle of a Spokane street, making obscene gestures at passing cars.

"It upsets me very much," Zigler said. "That was part of the agreement in the courtroom that day. This was supposed to have been to get them straight."

"Them" includes Stephanie's mother, Sharon Arger, 42, of Spokane, who said she is disabled by severe back pain. Zigler's lawyer, Jeffrey R. Smith, of Spokane, said Zigler is considering filing a civil lawsuit alleging wrongful death. Investigators are working to determine the source of the drugs that killed Tim, Smith said.

Arger said Zigler and his lawyer believe Stephanie got the drugs from Arger's cache of pain medication. But that's not true, said Arger. Stephanie did supply Tim with methadone, she acknowledged, but the girl got it from someone else.

"Everything was locked up. It wasn't mine," said Arger, who's also the mother of 5-year-old twins and a 2-year-old son. "I'm not this negligent person."

Stephanie has since posted dozens of clean drug tests and completed a General Equivalency Diploma, her mother said. Stephanie is "doing great," said Arger, who added she regrets that court rules have kept her from talking to Ken Zigler.

"I can't even say I'm sorry. I can't tell them who I am," she said. "I wanted to talk to them and I couldn't."

The only thing close to an apology came June 15, when Stephanie Davis was ordered to pay Zigler $2,310.64 in restitution, court records show.

"That was the cost of Tim's medical care and burial," Ken Zigler said quietly.

Zigler said he takes what comfort he can from the kids he's able to reach, young people in drug diversion programs who have a chance to make better choices.

"I'm hoping that I am personally touching kids' lives," he said.

Moving On Is Hard

Meanwhile, he's packing up the basement room of the rented home where Tim inked the names of his favorite bands—Metallica, Tool, Led Zeppelin—on the wall. For more than a year, Zigler couldn't bear to disturb anything. Now, he can't wait to pack it up and move on.

"We've got to get out of here," he said. "He would have been graduating. I feel like I'm saying, 'It's time to go, Tim.'"

The larger furniture went to a recycling center, where Zigler would be sure not to come across it. Smaller mementos of Tim's life are being packed into boxes.

One thing Zigler hasn't touched is a string of multicolored Christmas lights that Tim strung between two posts. Some of the bulbs are missing; several have burned out. But a few still glow.

"They've been going for a year and a half," the father said, his square shoulders slumping for just a moment.

"I just can't shut them off."

> *"But what if there were a vaccine to ease or even remove the rush associated with cocaine?"*

The Cocaine Vaccine May Be Effective

Kayt Sukel

Researchers are making progress toward the development of an effective cocaine vaccine, Kayt Sukel writes in the following viewpoint. The booster shot creates antibodies that block cocaine from entering the brain and other organs, preventing the physiological high, she asserts, which can suppress impulsive cravings and motivate addicts toward abstinence. This offers hope, but researchers still face the challenge of producing a stronger antibodies response, and complete recovery from addiction requires psychological treatment and time, the author suggests. Based in Hammersbach, Germany, Sukel is a writer and has contributed to the Washington Post.

As you read, consider the following questions:

1. Why is designing a vaccine for cocaine addiction desirable, according to Bridget Martell?

Kayt Sukel, "Cocaine Vaccine May Offer Alternative Therapy to Addicts," Dana.org, January 2010. Reprinted by permission.

2. How do the cocaine antibodies work in detail, as described by Sukel?

3. As explained by Sukel, why is immunization maintenance an issue?

Andrew Kent, 51, has been battling his addiction to cocaine for more than two decades. Though he has tried different recovery programs over the years, this Houston, Texas, native has relapsed time and time again.

Kent (a pseudonym to protect his family) says even a single hit can return him to the throes of addiction. "The drug just has you. You come off that high and it's not enough. It makes you want some more and more. And you'll do anything, even take from the ones you love, to get it."

But what if there were a vaccine to ease or even remove the rush associated with cocaine? What if booster shots could help addicts like Kent avoid relapses by taking away the physiological high that kept them coming back for more? Researchers at Yale University School of Medicine and the Baylor College of Medicine have completed a trial testing just such a vaccine. The study results were published in the October [2009] issue of the *Archives of General Psychiatry*.

Changes to the Brain from Addiction

In the past decade, neuroscientists have learned that there's a lot more to kicking a drug habit than just saying no. In fact, continued use of drugs like cocaine can make lasting changes to the brain.

"Over time, cocaine appears to damage the brain's natural reward mechanisms," says Eric Nestler, director of the [Friedman] Brain Institute at Mount Sinai School of Medicine and a member of the Dana Alliance for Brain Initiatives. "You continually blast the reward circuit and it becomes less sensitive.

So the person has this blunted reward circuit, doesn't feel good at all, and soon the fastest way just to feel normal is to take the drug."

The drug also alters the brain through subtle damage to the frontal cortex. "Cocaine diminishes the frontal cortex's ability to oversee executive control over impulses," Nestler says. "Everybody has impulses to do things they shouldn't, but they don't because it's not right or illegal. Drugs of abuse corrupt that ability to stop, and keep bringing addicts back to the drug."

Why a Vaccine?

Despite all that neuroscientists have learned about addiction-related changes to the brain, they are still years away from developing drugs or other therapies based on those findings. And current drugs, such as methadone for heroin use and disulfiram (Antabuse) for alcoholism, show inconsistent results—mainly because they only work as long as the addict is willing to take the drug.

"This is a population that is perfect for a therapeutic intervention that does not involve daily medication," says Bridget Martell, an associate director with Pfizer ... and adjunct faculty at Yale University School of Medicine. "If you look at the cited statistics of people with hypertension, only 50 percent of those patients will take medication. And when you are talking about a dependence on substances—the loss of the ability to function, hold down a job, have a relationship with family—you can only imagine what compliance might be."

Martell, lead author of the research paper, argues that a vaccine that blocks cocaine's access to the brain and other organs by using the body's natural immune response could be a great asset to addicts in recovery. "A vaccine can help these individuals develop antibodies and motivate them to stop using without needing to take a daily medication," she says. "And it does so without any negative side effects."

So Simple It's Sexy

Martell says the idea behind a vaccine is basic. "It's very simple biology—in fact, it's sexy because it's so simple," she says. "You have a small molecule that the body can't make antibodies to [cocaine] and stick it on to something else that will. In this case, we added it to the cholera toxin, which the immune system does respond to, and, in the process, makes anti-cocaine antibodies along with the anti-cholera ones."

Those anti-cocaine antibodies take up the drug molecules and then use the body's immune system to dispose of them before they cross blood-brain barriers. Since they don't reach the brain, they can't trigger the release of dopamine, the source of the drug's physiological high. Without the promise of the high, a person is much less motivated to take the drug again.

Thomas [R.] Kosten, Martell's colleague and a researcher at the Baylor College of Medicine, recruited addicts who were interested in recovery to test the vaccine. Of the 55 people who were given all five boosters, 38 percent developed enough of an antibody response to block entrance of cocaine to the brain and other organs. These individuals showed lower use of the drug over the course of the trial.

"It's the kind of result you hope for in a first-generation vaccine," Kosten says. "It's not as good as we hope to be—we know that we need to see higher levels of antibodies in more people—but we have newer vaccines in development that can get 5–6 times as much antibody response in animals now."

Challenges to Getting the Right Response

Berma Kinsey, a researcher developing different drug vaccines at Baylor, says the biggest challenge is finding a way to get that adequate antibody response. In this case, that may mean going back to the drawing board to develop methods that would make the vaccine stronger.

"Maybe something besides the cholera protein would give a better response," she says. "Or perhaps the adjuvant, the sub-

The Ultimate Weapons Against Addiction

Vaccines that would arm the immune system against addictive drugs and prevent them from making the user high are, potentially, the ultimate weapons against addiction. A cocaine vaccine is poised to enter its first large-scale clinical trial in humans this year [2008], and vaccines against nicotine, heroin and methamphetamine are also in development. In theory, these addiction vaccines work the same way as the traditional vaccines used to treat infectious diseases like measles and meningitis. But instead of targeting bacteria and viruses, the new vaccines zero in on addictive chemicals. Each of the proposed vaccines consists of drug molecules that have been attached to proteins from bacteria; it's the bacterial protein that sets off the immune reaction. Once a person has been vaccinated, the next time the drug is ingested, antibodies will latch onto it and prevent it from crossing from the bloodstream into the brain.

Jeneen Interlandi,
"What Addicts Need," Newsweek,
February 23, 2008.

stance given with the vaccine that tickles the immune response and makes it strong, needs to be adjusted. Or maybe we need a better system to deliver the vaccine. Any of these things could change the antibody response."

But beyond getting the contents of the vaccine right, there is also the question of maintenance. With a viral vaccine, the body will recognize the virus if a person is re-infected and will produce the proper antibody response. Not so with drug molecules.

"Your body hasn't made antibodies to just the cocaine—it's made them to some combination of the drug and the cholera toxin," Kosten says. "Just using the drug won't boost the immune response. You need to give several boosters to get the antibody levels to where you need them."

But perhaps the biggest challenge is addiction itself—which is not just a physiological disorder but also a psychological one. Both Martell and Kosten say the vaccine is not a panacea but a tool that can be used with existing psychosocial therapies.

"In general, it takes an addict about two years to turn their life around," Kosten says. "Addicts might get the vaccine booster every two months or so for those two years. But addiction is a chronic disease and, if a person relapsed, we could give them a single injection to push those antibodies back up again. It would be like having a little insurance policy available to help people get back on the straight and narrow."

Next Steps

Martell, Kosten and their colleagues are planning new trials of improved vaccines in hopes to attaining necessary, lasting antibody levels—and do so across wider populations of addicts. But even though the results are preliminary, Kent, for one, hopes that the vaccine will be made available soon.

"If there was a vaccine that would help me get this monkey off my back, I'd be number one on the list to try it," Kent says. "This is a disease that is destroying America. This is a disease that is still trying to destroy me. So if this vaccine does come out, I want to be first."

"In this study, immunization did not achieve complete abstinence from cocaine use."

The Cocaine Vaccine May Not Be Effective

Rachel Saslow

In the following viewpoint, Rachel Saslow contends that the experimental vaccine for cocaine and crack addiction may not completely suppress cravings. Known as TA-CD, the immunization has potential, but Saslow cites a recent study in which participants consumed more cocaine to counter the vaccination's effects. In fact, Saslow reports that researchers found ten times more cocaine in the participants' systems than before. She also expresses a concern that the public—particularly family members affected by addiction—misperceives a cocaine vaccine as a cure. The author is a staff reporter for the Washington Post.

As you read, consider the following questions:

1. According to Saslow, participants in the TA-CD study used more cocaine than usual after they had been vaccinated. What reasons does Saslow give for this increased use?

Rachel Saslow, "Testing of Cocaine Vaccine Shows It Does Not Fully Blunt Cravings for the Drug," *Washington Post*, January 5, 2010. Reprinted by permission.

2. According to Saslow, what do researchers know about why the vaccine did not make sufficient antibodies in a quarter of the study participants?

3. How does Margaret Haney address the ethical dilemma of administering crack cocaine to the study participants?

Scientists may have created a vaccine against cocaine addiction: a series of shots that changes the body's chemistry so that the drug can't enter the brain and provide a high.

The vaccine, called TA-CD, shows promise but could also be dangerous; some of the addicts participating in a study of the vaccine started doing massive amounts of cocaine in hopes of overcoming its effects, according to Thomas R. Kosten, the lead researcher on the study, which was published in the *Archives of General Psychiatry* in October [2009].

"After the vaccine, doing cocaine was a very disappointing experience for them," said Kosten, a professor of psychiatry and neuroscience at Baylor College of Medicine in Houston.

Nobody overdosed, but some of them had 10 times more cocaine coursing through their systems than researchers had encountered before, according to Kosten. He said some of the addicts reported to researchers that they had gone broke buying cocaine from multiple drug dealers, hoping to find a variety that would get them high.

Incomplete Abstinence

Of the 115 addicts in the study, 58 were given the vaccine, administered in a series of five shots over 12 weeks, while 57 received placebo injections. Six people dropped out before the end of the study. The researchers recruited the participants from a methadone-treatment program in West Haven, Conn., which made it possible to track them for the full 24 weeks of the study. The patients were addicted to cocaine and heroin; TA-CD is designed to work only on cocaine, including the crack form of the drug.

Like disease vaccines, TA-CD stimulates a person's immune system to produce antibodies. Of those who received all five vaccine injections, 38 percent reached antibody levels that were high enough to dull the effects of the drug. The antibodies stayed active for eight to 10 weeks after the last shot.

In the high-antibodies group, 53 percent stayed off cocaine more than half the time once they had built up immunity. That compares with 23 percent of those who produced fewer antibodies. The researchers monitored cocaine use through regular urinalysis.

"In this study, immunization did not achieve complete abstinence from cocaine use," Kosten said. "Previous research has shown, however, that a reduction in use is associated with a significant improvement in cocaine abusers' social functioning and thus is therapeutically meaningful."

About a quarter of those who received the vaccine did not make sufficient antibodies at all; Kosten isn't sure why.

"That's the million-dollar question," said Margaret Haney, a professor of clinical neuroscience at Columbia University Medical Center, who is also researching the cocaine vaccine though she was not involved in Kosten's study.

In October, the journal *Biological Psychiatry* published online an article by Haney that also tested the effects of TA-CD.

Through newspaper ads, Haney had recruited 15 cocaine-dependent men to participate in her study. (Only 10 stayed to the end.)

She and her colleagues gave crack cocaine to each man 39 times over 13 weeks while monitoring his heart. ("A nurse held a flame on the cocaine and participants were instructed to take one large inhalation and hold it as long as they would outside the laboratory," according to the study.) The researchers vaccinated each participant with TA-CD on weeks 1, 3, 5 and 9 and periodically asked him to fill out a survey about his mood.

Haney, who has been studying pharmacological treatment for cocaine addiction for 15 years, said she was surprised by how effective the medication was in blocking cocaine's effects. In the conclusion of her study, Haney suggested that the vaccine could help protect motivated treatment-seekers from relapse because if they slipped and used some cocaine, they wouldn't get high and trigger the craving for more drugs.

A Mistaken View

Regarding the ethics of giving laboratory-produced crack cocaine to the men, none of whom was seeking treatment for his addiction at the time of the study, Haney said that the benefits of developing a vaccine outweighed any potential harm. She said scientists have been doing these types of studies—funded by the federal government—for 20 years under safe, controlled conditions. "I sleep well at night because it's unethical not to do well-designed studies," she said.

A larger six-site clinical trial of the vaccine organized by Kosten is scheduled to start in the spring

The idea of developing a medication to block addiction has long been attractive: Disulfiram (now sold under the name Antabuse), which makes people ill if they drink alcohol, has been available for alcoholism since 1948. Kosten said he hasn't received any inquiries from drug companies wanting to manufacture a large-scale cocaine vaccine. (He and Haney are conducting research on TA-CD under an agreement with the private equity firm that controls the prospective vaccine; both of their studies were largely funded by the National Institutes of Health.)

According to the 2007 National Survey on Drug Use and Health, about 2.1 million Americans had used cocaine within the previous month.

Haney said she receives phone calls from desperate people asking where they can get the vaccine for a family member who is addicted.

"They have a mistaken view of how a vaccine might work, thinking of it as magic, where what it's doing, at best, is blunting the effects," Haney said. "They get very excited, and it's heartbreaking."

Periodical and Internet Sources Bibliography

The following articles have been selected to supplement the diverse views presented in this chapter.

Lisa Black	"Methadone Clinics Rise in Number, Raising Flags," *Chicago Tribune*, August 16, 2009.
Daniel Burke	"Catholic Needle Exchange Raises Moral Questions," *National Catholic Reporter*, February 10, 2010.
Katherine Harmon	"New Vaccine May Immunize Addicts from Cocaine's Pleasurable Effects," *Scientific American*, October 6, 2009.
Larry Hartstein and Todd Holcomb	"Drug Testing by High Schools Gets a Push from QB's Death," *Atlanta Journal-Constitution* (Atlanta, Georgia), July 10, 2007.
Hilary Hylton	"A Drug to End Drug Addiction," *Time*, January 9, 2008.
Donna Leinwand	"Principal: Drug-Testing Students Works," *USA Today*, July 12, 2006.
Kristin Pulatie	"The Legality of Drug-Testing Procedures for Pregnant Women," *American Medical Association Journal of Ethics*, January 2008.
Roni Caryn Rabin	"Cocaine Vaccine Is Developed, but It Does Not Keep Users from Wanting the Drug," *New York Times*, October 5, 2009.
Maia Szalavitz	"Needle Exchange and the New Drug Czar," STATS.org, December 3, 2008. http://stats.org.
Robert Tomsho	"New Study Suggests Alternative to Methadone Is More Effective," *Wall Street Journal*, August 20, 2009.

OPPOSING
VIEWPOINTS®
SERIES

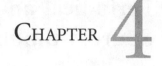

CHAPTER 4

Should Drug Laws Be Changed?

Chapter Preface

Portugal decriminalized the personal use of drugs in 2001, joining Italy and Spain to become the third nation in the European Union to do so. Instead of jail, users found guilty of possessing small amounts of illicit substances report to special authority commissions—including a social worker, mental health professional, and legal advisor—that determine treatment and counseling. The individual may decline rehabilitation without facing punishment. "The idea is to get away from punishment towards treatment,"[1] said Carlos Borges, a spokesman for the Portuguese government.

In April 2009 the libertarian think tank Cato Institute published a paper backing Portugal's drug policy and analyzing its first five years. The paper contends that after decriminalization, HIV transmissions decreased and twice as many addicts sought out treatment. Moreover, it reports that the lifetime use of marijuana for people fifteen and older reached a low of 10 percent, a record for the European Union. "The Portuguese have seen the benefits of decriminalization, and therefore there is no serious political push in Portugal to return to a criminalization framework,"[2] declares Glenn Greenwald, the author of the paper and former constitutional litigator for New York State. "Drug policy makers in the Portuguese government are virtually unanimous in their belief that decriminalization has enabled a far more effective approach to managing Portugal's addiction problems and other drug-related afflictions."

Still, some experts approach the paper's findings with caution. Criminologist Peter Reuter cites a global decline in marijuana use among adolescents and proposes that patterns of

---

1. BBC News, "Portugal Legalises Drug Use," July 7, 2000. http://news.bbc.co.uk.
2. Glenn Greenwald, "Drug Decriminalization in Portugal: Lessons for Creating Fair and Successful Drug Policies," April 2, 2009.

drug use fluctuate regardless of laws. Furthermore, Reuter suggests that the increased efforts of authorities to direct addicts to therapy extends the government's powers and may interfere with individual liberties. In the following chapter, the authors offer contrasting positions on drug policies in the United States, where personal use of all illicit substances is still criminalized.

> "A random adjustment will have severe
> negative consequences on the efforts of
> this nation's prosecutors to remove the
> destructive effects of crack and violence
> from our communities."

The Disparity in Crack and Powder Cocaine Sentences Is Necessary

Joseph I. Cassilly

Crack cocaine is more potent and destructive than powdered co-caine, and stricter federal sentencing for the former is justified, contends Joseph I. Cassilly in the following viewpoint. He maintains that crack has greater potential for abuse, with smokers outstripping the amounts of cocaine consumed by intranasal users. Therefore, Cassilly argues that crack addicts commit crimes to sustain their much more expensive habits, resulting in higher rates of homicide and prostitution. Critics allege that such sentencing is biased against black crack dealers, but Cassilly insists that the harm of crack addiction on communities is a greater

Joseph I. Cassilly, "Written Testimony of Joseph I. Cassilly, State's Attorney Harford County, Bel Air, Maryland and President-Elect, National District Attorneys Association, 'Federal Cocaine Sentencing Laws: Reforming the 100-to-1 Crack/Powder Disparity,' Subcommittee on Crime, Terrorism & Homeland Security, House Committee on Judiciary, United States House of Representatives," judiciary.house.gov, February 26, 2008. Reprinted by permission.

discrimination. The author is state's attorney for Harford County in Maryland and former president of the National District Attorneys Association.

As you read, consider the following questions:

1. How does the sentencing disparity serve the legal system, in Cassilly's opinion?

2. What evidence does Cassilly cite in support of his position that crack differs in effects than powdered cocaine?

3. Who pleads for greater punitive measures against crack dealers, according to the author?

I am testifying on behalf of the National District Attorneys Association [NDAA], the oldest and largest organization representing state and local prosecutors. Attached is a resolution adopted by NDAA regarding the sentencing disparity between crack and powder cocaine. NDAA agrees that some adjustment is warranted, but just as the 100:1 disparity cannot be justified by empirical data we believe that the proposed 1:1 realignment of federal penalties for crack versus powder cocaine also lacks any empirical or clinical evidence. A random adjustment will have severe negative consequences on the efforts of this nation's prosecutors to remove the destructive effects of crack and violence from our communities.

The cooperation of federal and state prosecutors and law enforcement that has developed over the years is due in large part to the interplay of federal and state laws. I have been a criminal prosecutor for over 30 years. My prosecutors and I work on one of the most active and successful task forces in Maryland. We actively operate with federal agents and prosecutors from the U.S. attorney for Maryland.

Maryland state statutes differentiate sentences between crack and powder cocaine offenders on a 9:1 ratio based on the amount that would indicate a major dealer. There is not a

100:1 difference in the sentences given to crack versus powder offenders. A DOJ [Department of Justice] report states, "A facial comparison of the guideline ranges for equal amounts of crack and powder cocaine reveals that crack penalties range from 6.3 times greater to approximately equal to powder sentences."

In recent years local prosecutors have brought hundreds of large quantity dealers for federal prosecution, primarily because of the discretion of federal prosecutors in dealing with these cases. This discretion allows for pleas to lesser amounts of cocaine or the option of not seeking sentence enhancements. The end result is that the majority of these cases are ultimately resolved by a guilty plea to a sentence below the statutory amount.

The practical effect of guilty pleas is that serious violent criminals are immediately removed from our communities, they spend less time free on bail or in pre-trial detention, civilian witnesses are not needed for trial or sentencing hearings and are therefore not subject to threats and intimidation and undercover officers are not called as witnesses: all of which would happen if we were forced to proceed with these cases in courts. Yet meaningful sentences are imposed, which punish the offender but also protect the community and allow it to heal from harm caused by these offenders. Moreover, the plea agreements often call for testimony against higher ups in the crack organization. It is critical that federal sentences for serious crack dealers remain stricter than state laws if this coordinated interaction is to continue.

First let me dispel some of the myths about controlled substance prosecutions that are propagated by those who would decriminalize the devastation caused by illegal drugs.

Myth 1: First-Time Offenders

Myth 1. Prisons are full of first-time offenders caught with small quantities of C.D.S. [controlled dangerous substances].

The fact is that in joint federal or state investigations small quantity dealers are delegated to state prosecutors for prosecution. First-time users are almost never sent to jail but are directed into treatment programs; a jail sentence is suspended to provide an incentive for them to participate in treatment.

Myth 2: Crack Versus Powder Cocaine

Myth 2. There is no difference between the effect of crack versus powder cocaine on the user.

In a study entitled "Crack Cocaine and Cocaine Hydrochloride: Are the Differences Myth or Reality?" by D.K. Hatsukami and M.W. Fischman, Department of Psychiatry, Division of Neurosciences, University of Minnesota, Minneapolis, it is stated,

> "The physiological and psychoactive effects of cocaine are similar regardless of whether it is in the form of cocaine hydrochloride or crack cocaine (cocaine base). However, evidence exists showing a greater abuse liability, greater propensity for dependence, and more severe consequences when cocaine is smoked (cocaine base) . . . compared with intranasal use (cocaine hydrochloride). The crucial variables appear to be the immediacy, duration, and magnitude of cocaine's effect, as well as the frequency and amount of cocaine used rather than the form of the cocaine."

Smoked cocaine results in the quickest onset and fastest penetration. Generally, smoked cocaine reaches the brain within 20 seconds; the effects last for about 30 minutes, at which time the user to avoid the effects of a "crash" reuses. The Drug Enforcement Administration's (DEA's) intelligence indicates that a crack user is likely to consume anywhere from 3.3 to 16.5 grams of crack a week, or between 13.2 grams and 66 grams per month.

Intranasally administered cocaine has a slower onset. The maximum psychotropic effects are felt within 20 minutes and the maximum physiological effects within 40 minutes. The effects from intranasally administered cocaine usually last for about 60 minutes after the peak effects are attained. A typical user snorts between two and three lines at a time and consumes about 2 grams per month.

Using these amounts, the cost per user per month for crack cocaine is between $1,300 and $6,600 as compared to a cost for powder cocaine of $200 per month; a 6.5 to 33:1 ratio in cost.

Myth 3: Associated Crimes and the Effect on the Community

Myth 3. There is no difference in the associated crimes and the effect on the community caused by crack as opposed to powder cocaine.

The inability to legitimately generate the large amount of money needed by a crack addict leads to a high involvement in crimes that can produce ready cash such as robbery and prostitution. Studies show crack cocaine use is more associated with systemic violence than powder cocaine use. One study found that the most prevalent form of violence related to crack cocaine abuse was aggravated assault. In addition, a 1998 study identified crack as the drug most closely linked to trends in homicide rates. Furthermore, crack is much more associated with weapons use than is powder cocaine: In FY [fiscal year] 2000, weapons were involved in 10.6% of powder convictions, and 21.3% of crack convictions.

One of the best documented links between increased crime and cocaine abuse is the link between crack use and prostitution. According to the authors of one study, "hypersexuality apparently accompanies crack use." In this study, 86.7% of women surveyed were not involved in prostitution in the year before starting crack use; one-third became involved in prostitution in the year after they began use. Women who were already involved in prostitution dramatically increased their in-

157

volvement after starting to use crack, with rates nearly four times higher than before beginning crack use.

One complaint about the sentencing disparity is that it discriminates against black crack dealers versus white powder dealers. Unfortunately, what most discriminates against our black citizens is the violence, degradation and community collapse that is associated with crack use and crack dealers and their organizations. It is the black homeowners who most earnestly plead with me, as a prosecutor, for strict enforcement and long prison sentences for crack offenders. The stop snitching video was made by black crack dealers in Baltimore to threaten black citizens with retaliation and death for fighting the dealers. A black family of five was killed by a fire bomb that was thrown into their home at the direction of crack dealers because they were reporting crack dealers on the street in front of their house.

Many federal, state and local prosecutors who struggle with the problems of crack can point out those areas in their jurisdictions with the highest violent crime rates are the same areas with the highest crack cocaine use.

Congress should consider that many persons serving federal crack sentences have received consideration from the prosecutors in return for a guilty plea (i.e., pleas to lesser amounts of cocaine or the option of not seeking sentence enhancements). Many criminals who could be affected by a retroactive application of a new sentencing scheme have already received the benefits of lower sentences and would get a second reduction. New sentencing hearings would mean that citizens from the communities the crack dealers once ruined would have to come forward to keep the sentences from being cut.

The nation's prosecutors urge Congress to adopt a sentencing scheme with regard to the destruction caused by crack cocaine to our communities. If there is a need to reduce the disparity between crack and powder cocaine then perhaps the solution is to increase sentences for powder cocaine.

"The crack/powder [cocaine] disparity is causing great harm to families, taxpayers, and the criminal justice system."

The Disparity in Crack and Powder Cocaine Sentences Is Ineffective and Unfair

Bill Piper

Bill Piper is director of the Office of National Affairs for the Drug Policy Alliance. In the following viewpoint, Piper asserts that the disparity in the federal law for crack and powder cocaine offenses must be reformed. For instance, the author claims that smoking and snorting cocaine have similar physiological and psychoactive effects, negating the need for unequal punishment. More importantly, the current policy and target of low-level offenders oppresses black Americans, despite the fact that two-thirds of crack users are white, he adds. Piper puts forth that not only the sentencing disparity be eliminated, but also that the federal government take extensive measures to restore communities unfairly affected by the drug war.

Bill Piper, "Written Testimony of Bill Piper, Director of National Affairs, Drug Policy Alliance, 'Federal Cocaine Sentencing Laws: Reforming the 100-to-1 Crack/Powder Disparity,' Subcommittee on Crime, Terrorism & Homeland Security, House Committee on Judiciary, United States House of Representatives," drugpolicy.org, February 26, 2008. Reprinted by permission.

As you read, consider the following questions:

1. How was the current federal policy on crack cocaine shaped, in Piper's opinion?

2. How have high incarceration rates of black Americans under the sentencing disparity affected their communities, as stated by the author?

3. In the author's view, what steps should Congress take to assist in the recovery of affected communities?

The Drug Policy Alliance (DPA) is the leading organization promoting alternatives to the failed war on drugs. Headquartered in New York City, DPA also has offices in Berkeley, Los Angeles, Sacramento, San Francisco, Santa Fe, Trenton, and Washington, D.C. Our mission is to institute a new bottom line for U.S. drug policy, one that focuses on reducing the problems associated with both drugs and the war on drugs. In 2005 the Drug Policy Alliance spearheaded a successful campaign in Connecticut to eliminate that state's crack/powder [cocaine] sentencing disparity, and we're currently working in Ohio to do the same there.

DPA strongly supports the Drug Sentencing Reform and Cocaine Kingpin Trafficking Act, the only bill in the Senate that would completely eliminate the crack/powder sentencing disparity. This disparity has devastated black communities, wasted taxpayer dollars, and undermined public safety by encouraging federal law enforcement agencies to target low-level drug law offenders instead of major crime syndicates. While we commend Senators [Jeff] Sessions and [Orrin] Hatch for their leadership on this issue, we are disappointed that neither of their bills fully eliminates the disparity.

Reducing the 100-to-1 crack/powder disparity to 20-to-1, as the Sessions (S. 1383) and Hatch (S. 1685) bills do, is like amending the Constitution's three-fifths clause to make African Americans fourth-fifths citizens, or integrating 60% of public establishments instead of all of them. Policy makers should seek to eliminate discrimination not just reduce it.

Additionally, unlike the [former senator Joe] Biden or Hatch bill, the Sessions bill lowers the amount of powder cocaine it takes to trigger a federal mandatory minimum sentence. This would encourage the U.S. Justice Department to target low-level powder cocaine offenders instead of high-level offenders. To the bill's credit it would significantly reduce racial disparities for African Americans, but by lowering powder thresholds it would most likely increase racial disparities for Hispanics—an unacceptable trade-off.

When the crack/powder sentencing disparity was enacted into law in the 1980s, crack cocaine was believed to be more addictive and more dangerous than powder cocaine. Copious amounts of research, including a recent study by the U.S. Sentencing Commission, have shown that the myths first associated with crack cocaine, and the basis for the harsher sentencing scheme, were erroneous or exaggerated. For over two decades, powder cocaine and crack cocaine offenders have been sentenced differently at the federal level, even though scientific evidence, including a major study published in the *Journal of the American Medical Association*, has proven that crack and powder cocaine have similar physiological and psychoactive effects on the human body.

Racial Disparities

Perhaps no other single federal policy is more responsible for gross racial disparities in the federal criminal justice system than the crack/powder sentencing disparity. Even though two-thirds of crack cocaine users are white, more than 80% of those convicted in federal court for crack cocaine offenses are African American. Moreover, two-thirds of those convicted have only a low-level involvement in the drug trade. Less than 2% of federal crack defendants are high-level suppliers of cocaine. Taxpayer money should be spent wisely, and concentrating federal law enforcement and criminal justice resources on arresting and incarcerating low-level, largely nonviolent offenders has done nothing to reduce the problems associated with substance abuse.

Furthermore, the current sentencing policy, and the targeting of low-level offenders, has proven devastating for families and communities that suffer high incarceration rates. According to a 2006 report by the American Civil Liberties Union, 1 in 14 black children has a parent in prison, and approximately 1.4 million black men—13% of all adult African American males—are disenfranchised because of felony drug convictions. Single-parent homes, unemployment, disillusionment with the justice system and stigmas from felony convictions and incarcerations can contribute to the degradation of already disadvantaged communities and increase crime rates. The U.S. Sentencing Commission has noted that even "perceived improper racial disparity fosters disrespect for and lack of confidence in the criminal justice system."

Most U.S. states do not differentiate between crack and powder cocaine when it comes to sentencing and neither should the federal government. The Drug Policy Alliance urges members of the Crime and Drugs Subcommittee to stand up for justice and public safety by quickly passing the Drug Sentencing Reform and Cocaine Kingpin Trafficking Act. We also urge you to rethink federal drug policy more broadly.

The Excesses of U.S. Drug Policy

More than half of all people incarcerated in federal prison are there for drug law violations, and through various law enforcement grant programs the federal government encourages the mass incarceration of nonviolent drug offenders at the local and state level as well. Police make more than 1.8 million drug arrests in the U.S. every year (nearly 700,000 for nothing more than simple marijuana possession). Those arrested are separated from their loved ones, branded criminals, denied jobs, and in many cases prohibited from accessing public assistance for life. The United States incarcerates more of its citizens for drug violations than all of Western Europe incarcerates for all crimes combined (and Western Europe has 100 million more people).

Yet despite spending hundreds of billions of dollars and arresting millions of Americans, illegal drugs remain cheap, potent and widely available in every community, and the harms associated with them continue to mount. Meanwhile, the war on drugs is creating problems of its own—broken families, racial disparities, and the erosion of civil liberties. The crack/powder disparity may be one of the worst excesses of U.S. drug policy but it is still just the tip of the iceberg.

In a recent op-ed in New Orleans' *Times-Picayune*, former ACLU [American Civil Liberties Union] executive director and current Drug Policy Alliance president Ira Glasser makes the case that the war on drugs is one of the major civil rights issues of our day.

> [T]he racially discriminatory origin of most [drug] laws is reinforced by the disparate impact they have on racially targeted drug felons. In the states of the Deep South, 30 percent of black men are barred from voting because of felony convictions. But all of them are nonetheless counted as citizens for the purpose of determining congressional representation and electoral college votes. The last time something like this happened was during slavery, when three-fifths of slaves were counted in determining congressional representation.
>
> Just as Jim Crow laws were a successor system to slavery in the attempt to keep blacks subjugated, so drug prohibition has become a successor system to Jim Crow laws in targeting black citizens, removing them from civil society and then barring them from the right to vote while using their bodies to enhance white political power in Congress and the electoral college.

"AH, FALL...KIDS IN SCHOOL... FOOTBALL...UTTER FUTILITY AND HYPOCRISY OF THE "DRUG WAR" FILLING THE AIR..."

More Needs to Be Done

Eliminating the crack/powder cocaine sentencing disparity is a good start in tearing down this new Jim Crow, but more needs to be done.

As I told members of the House Subcommittee on Crime, Terrorism and Homeland Security during Chairman [Bobby] Scott's Crime Policy Summit last year [in 2007], Congress should restore the right to vote to Americans who have served their time; require law enforcement agencies receiving federal funding to document their arrests, seizures, and searches by race and ethnicity; repeal policies that ban former drug law offenders from receiving student loans, public housing and TANF [Temporary Assistance for Needy Families]; and raise the threshold amount of drugs it takes to trigger federal mandatory minimum sentences to encourage the Justice Department to prosecute high-level traffickers.

If you would like to be bold, pass legislation requiring federal agencies to set short- and long-term goals for reducing the problems associated with both drugs and punitive drug policies. The Office of National Drug Control Policy (ONDCP), for instance, is already statutorily required to set annual goals for reducing drug use and drug availability. Why not also require the agency to set annual goals for reducing overdose deaths, the spread of HIV/AIDS from injection drug use, the number of Americans who cannot vote because of a felony conviction, and other criteria. If ONDCP, the Justice Department and other agencies were graded and funded in part on their ability to reduce racial disparities in the criminal justice system, then those agencies would probably be supporting crack/powder reform instead of opposing it or standing on the sidelines.

Reforming federal cocaine sentencing laws should unquestionably be the Crime and Drugs Subcommittee's top priority this year. The crack/powder disparity is causing great harm to families, taxpayers, and the criminal justice system. Eliminating it would be one of the biggest civil rights accomplishments of this decade. The disparity, however, is just one part of a larger set of failed drug policies that need to be reformed.

> *"Drug courts, 'the most effective criminal justice strategy for dealing with alcohol and other drug offenders,' only serve 5 percent of the criminal population."*

Drug Courts Are a Promising Solution to the Drug Problem

Peggy Fulton Hora

Peggy Fulton Hora is a retired judge who served twenty-one years in the California Superior Court. In the following viewpoint, she proposes that drug courts are effective at dealing with chemical dependency. Incarceration and probation are not deterrents to addiction, Hora states. In fact, she claims that the one-size-fits-all approach of mandatory sentencing is not appropriate, but the flexibility in a drug court assesses whether a defendant would benefit more from treatment and rehabilitation. As the system continues to spread across the country, Hora suggests that peer accreditation and developing standards will help new courts follow the principles of drug courts.

As you read, consider the following questions:

1. How does Hora describe her first year as a judge?

Peggy Fulton Hora, "Through a Glass Gavel: Predicting the Future of Drug Treatment Courts," *Future Trends in State Courts*, September 2009, p. 134–139. Reprinted by permission.

2. What is the author's opinion of juvenile drug courts?

3. In Hora's words, what reasons indicate that the public endorses drug courts?

I came to the bench with a background in civil law so, of course, my first assignment was to the criminal division. I spent the first year as a judge sentencing people convicted of crimes; telling them not to use drugs; telling them not to drink alcohol; and telling them to complete alcohol-awareness or substance-abuse programs, and, much to my surprise, they disobeyed my orders. I was shocked. If a judge told me not to drink anymore, well there goes the wine cellar. No problem.

As the year wore on and I saw the same people over and over, I began to ask questions, I wanted to know why these people behaved as they did. I wanted to know how to be more effective in my sentencing, I could see 20 years on the bench looming before me where I continued using ineffective methods. I needed to understand how to do a better job so I started taking chemical dependency courses at my local college and learning everything I could about alcoholism and other addictions.

As luck would have it, other judges were asking similar questions and wondering how to do be more effective. In 1989 the first drug court opened in Miami; I chaired the committee that developed the second one in the United States, the first in California, three years later. I was one of the 100 people who gathered in Miami and created the National Association of Drug Court Professionals [NADCP] in 1994. This year, 2009, marks the 20th anniversary of drug courts, and I will be speaking at NADCP's 15th annual training conference, as I have done almost every year before.

I cochaired the first state conference on drugs in California and the first that was interdisciplinary. Never before had judges sat down with prosecutors, defense counsel, treatment providers, and others in a professional education setting to ex-

plore how we could work together to improve the lives of people in trouble. I helped develop a weeklong course on alcohol and other drugs for California judges and for the National Judicial College [NJC]. Training on addiction is now mandatory at California's judicial college. And I still teach a four-day course at NJC on co-occurring substance abuse and mental health disorders.

I've made scores of presentations all over the United States and in other countries on substance abuse issues and have a particular interest in cultural competence and co-occurring disorders. The U.S. State Department has sent me to Israel and Chile to talk to judges about drug treatment courts, and I will spend 12 weeks in Australia advising the government on issues of therapeutic jurisprudence and restorative justice in 2009–10.

I have written 16 articles for journals and law reviews on drug treatment courts, other problem-solving courts, and the interplay between substance abuse and the justice system. You might say I have found my passion. Having been fortunate to see the beginning of this justice revolution where there are now more than 3,100 problem-solving courts, I decided to take a look into my crystal ball—that is, crystal gavel—to see what the future of drug treatment courts will look like.

Drug Treatment Courts Will Go to Scale and Serve Every Individual

Just as the Center for Substance Abuse Treatment (CSAT) has adopted "treatment on demand," so are advocates saying drug courts must "go to scale." These combined themes mean that every person who needs substance abuse treatment inside or outside of the criminal justice setting should get it. Drug treatment courts, "the most effective criminal justice strategy for dealing with alcohol and other drug offenders," only serve 5 percent of the criminal population. So, how then can we justify increasing funding for problem-solving courts in this economic climate? The fact that most drug treatment courts are in urban areas has recently been credited with sharply reducing the number of African Americans who are incarcerated. If this trend continues, the large numbers of Americans who are currently disenchanted with a system they see as racist may be reduced. This will increase trust and confidence in the judiciary, and this situation alone could justify the expansion of such courts. However, there are hard economic facts that support expansion as well. [According to the NADCP,] "A $250 million [up from $15.2 million in 2008 and an average of $40 million since the first federal funding] annual federal investment would reap staggering savings, with an estimated annual return of as much as $840 million in net benefits from avoided criminal justice and victimization costs alone." Treating the proper criminal justice target population would save $2.14 for every $1.00 spent totaling $1.17 *billion* in savings annually. Finally, drug courts are one of the most effective strategies in reducing recidivism according to Roger Warren, president emeritus of the National Center for State Courts. "Rigorous scientific studies and meta-analyses have found that drug courts significantly reduce recidivism among drug court participants in comparison to similar but nonparticipating offenders, with effect sizes ranging from 10% to 70%."

Every innovation—from cars to computers—started small, and their naysayers said cost would prevent the average person from owning one. However, once the product is mass-produced, there is no need to repeat the initial investment. So, too, is the case of drug courts because, if brought to scale, they can spread small incremental returns over large numbers of cases. Drug courts will be cheaper and more efficient. The 2009 Omnibus Appropriations Bill allocates $63.9 million for drug courts, a 250 percent increase over last year and the largest appropriation in the history of drug courts. Based on both the economic and social benefits of drug treatment courts, funding on both the federal and state level will continue to expand.

Current Promising Practices of Other Problem-Solving Courts

Drug courts, it turns out, are only the beginning of the justice system revolution that started 20 years ago. The first drug treatment court in Miami in 1989 spawned a movement of adult drug courts in the United States, which, as of December 2008, now number 2,301, plus some 1,191 other types of courts using similar principles. These problem-solving courts, as they have come to be known, now number more than 3,100 in the United States, including at least one drug court in every state; federal district courts; and over 70 tribal healing-to-wellness courts. There are problem-solving courts in some 20 other countries as well. Evaluations of the second wave of problem-solving courts are not nearly as numerous as those of adult drug treatment courts, but many show promise.

The verdict is in on drug treatment courts. It has been proven beyond a reasonable doubt that drug courts work. Slightly less clear is the efficacy of *family-dependency drug treatment courts* where parents are at risk of losing custody of their children and agree to enter into substance abuse treatment as part of their reunification plan. There have been fewer analyses, but we can say with clear and convincing evidence (or 75 percent certainty) that these courts are helpful in retention and completion of parents in treatment; result in less time for the children in out-of-home placements; and provide greater rates of reunification of families.

The more than 300 *driving-while-impaired (DWI) courts* operating in the country do not have sufficient evaluation literature yet, and studies that have been published show mixed results. There has been one recent, quasi-experimental study but with quite small samples. DWI courts can only be considered as likely to be effective in reducing DWI recidivism.

Juvenile drug courts, where the minor is the participant, show extremely mixed outcomes. There have been two meta-analyses of evaluations, but both showed null results. This may be because less is known about the treatment of juveniles, juveniles themselves are very difficult to manage, or the adult drug court model may not be appropriate for juveniles. Likewise there is a dearth of scientific evidence on the efficacy of mental health courts—diversion programs to keep people with mental disabilities from going to jail or prison. We can say that both these courts are likely to help children who are in trouble with alcohol or other drugs or people with mental health issues; clearly, both areas are ripe for more research to determine efficacy.

The problem-solving approach has been applied to all manner of behaviors from gambling to domestic violence and to special classes of people like women, college students or, as in the latest initiative, veterans. The first *veterans court* began in Buffalo, New York, in June 2008, and these courts are now found in Alaska, California, and Oklahoma, with 20 other states planning to start them. In addition to all the "specialty courts" mentioned thus far, there are *community courts and reentry drug courts*. But in the future we will see a different type of court. The need for these dedicated courts will eventually fade as more judges learn and practice problem-solving techniques in their courtrooms. Eventually, every court will be a problem-solving court, and every judge will use motivational interviewing and evidence-based sentencing while presiding over people's lives, not just "cases."

Evidence-Based Sentencing Will Be Employed by Every Judge in Every Court

The move toward evidence-based practices has been evolving since the 1990s. Drug treatment courts were among the first to apply some of these doctrines on a large scale. In the field of substance abuse and mental health treatment, interventions that have been rated and peer reviewed are eligible for inclusion in the National Registry of Evidence-Based Programs and Practices (NREPP) at the Substance Abuse and Mental Health

Services Administration (SAMHSA). The goal of the registry is to "improve access to information on tested interventions and thereby reduce the lag time [currently 12 years] between the creation of scientific knowledge and its practical application in the field" (NREPP Web site). Similar to SAMHSA's initiative, evidence-based sentencing is evolving to use problem-solving techniques to reduce recidivism and promote fairness in the courtroom. The chief justices of the 50 states were surveyed by the National Center for State Courts in 2006, and among their major concerns were 1) high rates of recidivism; 2) ineffectiveness of traditional probation supervision in reducing recidivism; 3) absence of effective community corrections programs; and 4) restrictions on judicial discretion that limit the ability of judges to sentence more fairly and effectively.

Traditionally, judges were given limited tools in their criminal justice kit—incarceration and probation. Yet we know that jail or prison is ineffective as a deterrent for many crimes, and without treatment for the underlying causes of criminal behaviors, recidivism rates are off the charts. Seventy percent of drug offenders, for instance, are rearrested within three years of release from custody. One out of every 31 adults is under supervision by probation or parole in the United States, and caseloads so far exceed every standard that mass supervision is no longer an effective strategy.

Modern practices rely on scientifically proven risk-assessment tools, so the level of interventions afforded each individual is tailored to their needs and takes multiple factors, not just prior arrest history and the nature of the crime, into account. Thomas Jefferson is credited with saying, "Nothing is more unequal than the equal treatment of unequal people." Imposing conditions beyond those directly related to an offender's risks or needs is ineffective, is wasteful, and may be perceived as unfair, thus eroding confidence and trust in the judiciary.

Risk-assessment instruments measure the likelihood that a defendant will reoffend so that resources can go to the highest-risk offender, and low-risk offenders can be managed with fines, volunteer work, and other low-level sanctions. Clearly, the one-size-fits-all requirements imposed by mandatory sentences are at best outdated and ineffective, costly, and often counterproductive to the community and the individual. There will be a move away from mandatory sentencing as was recently done in New York State with the elimination of the "draconian Rockefeller drug laws." We will shift toward evidence-based sentencing that will include the problem-solving approach in all courts.

Drug Courts Will Be Peer Accredited and Employ "Industry" Standards

What makes a drug court a drug court? The first use of the term "drug court" arose in Chicago, where a special "rocket docket" was initiated to send drug offenders to prison faster. The founders of the drug-treatment-court movement had something else entirely in mind in 1994 when the National Association of Drug Court Professionals was founded. They envisioned a process of court-supervised interventions that kept people *out* of jail and prison and fostered their recovery from the disease of addiction. In 1997, with the help of a grant from the Department of Justice, NADCP attempted to define a drug court for the first time. The resulting document, *Defining Drug Courts: The Key Components* (NADCP Drug Court Standards Committee, 1997), has become the Rosetta Stone for drug courts both nationally and internationally. Each "Key Component" is accompanied by "Performance Benchmarks," which seek to further refine the principles set forth in the document. "While each drug court should maintain fidelity to the drug court model, the design and structure of drug courts are developed at the local level to reflect the unique strengths, circumstances, and capacities of each community." Just as one of the strengths of the entire movement

Linking Supervision and Treatment

Drug courts offer an alternative to incarceration, which, by itself, has not been effective in breaking the cycle of drugs and crime. Treatment has been shown to work—if substance abusers stick with it; however, between 80 and 90 percent of conventional drug treatment clients drop out before 12 months, the period generally found to be the minimum effective duration. By providing a structure that links supervision and treatment, drug courts exert legal pressure on defendants to enter and remain in treatment long enough to realize benefits. More than two-thirds of participants who begin treatment through a drug court complete it in a year or more—a sixfold increase in retention compared with programs outside the justice system.

Alberto R. Gonzales, Regina B. Schofield, Glenn R. Schmitt,
"Drug Courts: The Second Decade," June 2006.

has been to eschew an imposed template of strict rules and regulations to define courts, this has led to some courts calling themselves drug courts that may not adhere to the underlying principles. To combat this issue, the field will develop standards and a peer-accreditation process to be sure that systems operating as drug courts truly do adhere to drug court principles. This process would allow funders to be more confident their money is going into the right budgets, and it would increase integrity for the whole justice system.

Wide Acceptance of Problem-Solving Courts Will Continue to Be the Norm

The first national meeting of drug court professionals in Miami in 1994 was attended by about 100 judges, prosecutors, defense counsel, treatment providers, and probation officers who shared a vision of a better way to handle drug cases. There was no identified underlying jurisprudential basis for what they were doing, and often no legislation specifically authorizing it. But these were the innovators, the pioneers, the "early adapters" who started the drug-treatment-court movement. Six years later, there were 500 drug courts; 1,000 by 2002; and more than 2,000 today. The movement came into its own when drug courts received the imprimatur of the Conference of Chief Justices (CCJ) in a resolution approved 50-0 at its 2000 annual meeting. This commitment was reaffirmed in 2004 and expanded to include support of mental health courts in 2006. In its commentary accompanying these resolutions, CCJ and the Conference of State Court Administrators (COSCA) said they would encourage the "broad integration over the next decade of the principles and methods employed in the problem-solving courts," support national and local education and training on the principles and methods, and advocate for the resources necessary to advance and apply the principles and methods of problem-solving courts.

Federal legislation that funded the first drug courts began under the administration of President Bill Clinton. He said, "Three-quarters of the growth in the number of federal prison inmates is due to drug crimes. Building new prisons will only go so far. Drug courts and mandatory testing and treatment are effective. I have seen drug courts work. I know they ... make a difference." Presidential support continued and funding increased under President George W. Bush, who said, "Drug courts are an effective and cost-efficient way to help nonviolent drug offenders commit to a rigorous drug treatment program in lieu of prison." And President Barack Obama not only made campaign promises about the expansion of drug courts, but also increased the 2009 drug court appropriation by 250 percent. Presidents Clinton and Bush chose directors of the White House Office of National Drug Control Policy [ONDCP] who supported drug courts, and this endorsement was best articulated by Director John Walters: "Drug courts are a vital, essential element of our National Drug Control Strategy. While offering incentives to stay off drugs, they hold individuals accountable and simultaneously deal with the deadly disease of addiction. America is better off because of drug courts." Finally, when introducing Seattle Police Chief Gil Kerlikowske in March 2009, President Obama's choice for ONDCP director, Vice President Joseph Biden said, "That's why the drug courts I spoke about are so important—as are prisoner reentry programs—because these can serve as the light at the end of a tunnel, a very long, long, dark tunnel, for those who are stuck in the cycle of drug addiction and incarceration."

Drug courts have support from the highest level of the judiciary and the federal government, but equally as important is their support by the public. In many ways, the citizenry was ahead of the politicians in support of treatment over incarceration. Voters are tired of building more prisons at the expense of education budgets and social programs. They realize "smart on crime" makes much more sense than "tough on crime," and the appropriate way to "get tough" is to demand treatment for those offenders who have addictions. Hazelden, one of the oldest treatment centers in the United States, found in a recent survey that 77 percent of those questioned believe that substance abuse treatment is effective, 79 percent believe the "war on drugs" was not effective, 83 percent would like to see more prevention, and 83 percent favor treatment over incarceration for addicted offenders. Given the outcomes achieved by drug courts and the fact that almost every family is touched by addictions, there is no reason to believe that public support will fade. In fact, just the opposite is true: Increased funding and increased participation of criminal defendants in drug treatment courts will advance both the government's and the public's support of these innovative courts.

> *"While drug courts can claim success as measured by the metrics embraced by the therapeutic–criminal justice complex, they appear deeply perverse and wrongheaded to people who do not embrace that model."*

Drug Courts Are Not a Solution to the Drug Problem

Phillip Smith

Drug War Chronicle is the publication of StoptheDrugWar.org, an advocate for policy reform. In the following viewpoint, Phillip Smith contends that many harm reductionists and addiction specialists oppose drug courts. According to Smith, treatment for drug addiction should be voluntary, not enforced; some drug courts reject methadone-assisted rehabilitation; judges may not understand addiction as a chronic condition; and some drug courts are under attack for denying due process rights to defendants. While drug courts are better than prison for addicts, Smith believes that chemical dependency should not be confronted with sanctions.

Phillip Smith, "Twenty Years of Drug Courts—Results and Misgivings," *Drug War Chronicle*, no. 580, April 9, 2009. stopthedrugwar.org. Reprinted by permission.

As you read, consider the following questions:

1. How do drug courts add to the problems in the criminal justice system, as described in the viewpoint?

2. What is Kevin Zeese's view of drug courts and criminal justice?

3. As stated by Delaney Ellison, what is the dilemma of the poor in drug courts?

The drug court phenomenon celebrates its 20th birthday this year [2009]. The first drug court, designed to find a more effective way for the criminal justice system to deal with drug offenders, was born in Miami in 1989 under the guidance of then local prosecutor Janet Reno. Since then, drug courts have expanded dramatically, with their number exceeding 2,000 today, including at least one in every state.

According to Urban Institute estimates, some 55,000 people are currently in drug court programs. The group found that another 1.5 million arrestees would probably meet the criteria for drug dependence and would thus be good candidates for drug courts.

The notion behind drug courts is that providing drug treatment to some defendants would lead to better outcomes for them and their communities. Unlike typical criminal proceedings, drug courts are intended to be collaborative, with judges, prosecutors, social workers, and defense attorneys working together to decide what would be best for the defendant and the community.

Drug courts can operate either by diverting offenders into treatment before sentencing or by sentencing offenders to prison terms and suspending the sentences providing they comply with treatment demands. They also vary in their criteria for eligibility: Some may accept only nonviolent, first-time offenders considered to be addicted, while others may have broader criteria.

Such courts rely on sanctions and rewards for their clients, with continuing adherence to treatment demands met with a loosening of restrictions and relapsing into drug use subjected to ever harsher punishments, typically beginning with a weekend in jail and graduating from there. People who fail drug court completely are then either diverted back into the criminal justice system for prosecution or, if they have already been convicted, sent to prison.

Strange and Contradictory

Drug courts operate in a strange and contradictory realm that embraces the model of addiction as a disease needing treatment, yet punishes failure to respond as if it were a moral failing. No other disease is confronted in such a manner. There are no diabetes courts, for example, where one is placed under the control of the criminal justice system for being sick and subject to "flash incarceration" for eating forbidden foods.

Conceptual dilemmas notwithstanding, drug courts have been extensively studied, and the general conclusion is that, within the parameters of the therapeutic/criminal justice model, they are successful. A recently released report from the Sentencing Project is the latest addition to the literature, or, more accurately, review of the literature.

In the report, "Drug Courts: A Review of the Evidence," the group concluded that:

- Drug courts have generally been demonstrated to have positive benefits in reducing recidivism.

- Evaluations of the cost effectiveness of drug courts have generally found benefits through reduced costs of crime or incarceration.

- Concern remains regarding potential "net-widening" effects of drug courts by drawing in defendants who might not otherwise have been subject to arrest and prosecution.

"What you have with drug courts is a program that the research has shown time and time again works," said Chris Deutsch, associate director of communications for the National Association of Drug Court Professionals in suburban Washington, D.C. "We all know the problems facing the criminal justice system with drug offenders and imprisonment. We have established incentives and sanctions as an important part of the drug court model because they work," he said. "One of the reasons drug courts are expanding so rapidly," said Deutsch, "is that we don't move away from what the research shows works. This is a scientifically validated model."

"There is evidence that in certain models there is success in reducing recidivism, but there is not a single model that works," said Ryan King, coauthor of the Sentencing Project report. "We wanted to highlight common factors in success, such as having judges with multiple turns in drug court and who understand addiction, and building on graduated sanctions, but also to get people to understand the weaknesses."

"Drug courts are definitely better than going to prison," said Theshia Naidoo, a staff attorney for the Drug Policy Alliance, which has championed a less coercive treatment-not-jail program in California's Proposition 36, "but they are not the be-all and end-all of addressing drug abuse. They may be a step forward in our current prohibitionist system, but when you look at their everyday operations, it's pretty much criminal justice as usual."

That was one of the nicest things said about drug courts by harm reductionists and drug policy reformers contacted this week by the *Chronicle*. While drug courts can claim success as measured by the metrics embraced by the therapeutic–criminal justice complex, they appear deeply perverse and wrongheaded to people who do not embrace that model.

Remarks by Kevin Zeese of Common Sense for Drug Policy hit many of the common themes. "If drug courts result in more people being caught up in the criminal justice system, I

Sweeping Conclusions

Proponents of drug courts often claim that numerous studies have conclusively demonstrated that drug courts work. Besides the numerous problems ... data simply does not support these sweeping conclusions. Completion rates for many drug court studies range from 25 to 66 percent. Thus, up to 2/3 of the initial participants *do not complete treatment.*

Steven K. Erickson,
"The Drug Court Fraud,"
Criminal Justice Legal Foundation, 2006.

do not see them as a good thing," he said. "The US has one out of 31 people in prison on probation or on parole, and that's a national embarrassment more appropriate for a police state than the land of the free. If drug courts are adding to that problem, they are part of the national embarrassment, not the solution."

But Zeese was equally disturbed by the therapeutic–criminal justice model itself. "Forcing drug treatment on people who happen to get caught is a very strange way to offer health care," he observed. "We would see a greater impact if treatment on request were the national policy and sufficient funds were provided to treatment services so that people who wanted treatment could get it quickly. And, the treatment industry would be a stronger industry if they were not dependent on police and courts to be sending them 'clients'—by force—and if instead they had to offer services that people wanted."

For Zeese, the bottom line was: "The disease model has no place in the courts. Courts don't treat disease, doctors and health professionals do."

A Hammer Imposing Sanctions

In addition to such conceptual and public policy concerns, others cited more specific problems with drug court operations. "In Connecticut, the success of drug courts depends on educated judges," said Robert Heimer of the Yale School of Public Health. "For example, in some parts of the state, judges refused to send defendants with opioid addiction to methadone programs. This dramatically reduced the success of the drug courts in these parts of the state compared to parts of the state where judges referred people to the one proven medically effective form of treatment for their addiction."

Heimer's complaint about the rejection of methadone maintenance therapy was echoed on the other side of the Hudson River by upstate New York drug reformer Nicolas Eyle of Reconsider: Forum on Drug Policy. "Most, if not all, drug courts in New York abhor methadone and maintenance treatment in general," he noted. "This is troubling because the state's recent Rockefeller law reforms have a major focus on treatment in lieu of prison, suggesting that more and more hapless people will be forced to enter treatment they may not need or want. Then the judge decides what type of treatment they must have, and when they don't achieve the therapeutic goals set for them they'll be hauled off to serve their time."

Still, said Heimer, "Such courts can work if appropriate treatment options are available, but if the treatment programs are bad, then it is unlikely that courts will work. In such cases, if the only alternative is then incarceration, there is little reason for drug courts. If drug court personnel think their program is valuable, they should be consistently lobbying for better drug treatment in their community. If they are not doing this, then they are contributing to the circumstances of their own failure, and again, the drug user becomes the victim if the drug court personnel are not doing this."

Even within the coerced treatment model, there are more effective approaches than drug courts, said Naidoo. "Drug courts basically have a zero tolerance policy, and many judges just don't understand addiction as a chronic relapsing condition, so if there is a failed drug test, the court comes in with a hammer imposing a whole series of sanctions. A more effective model would be to look at the overall context," she argued. "If the guy has a dirty urine, but has found a job, gotten housing, and is reunited with his family, maybe he shouldn't be punished for the relapse. The drug court would punish him."

Other harm reductionists were just plain cynical about drug courts. "I guess they work in reducing the drug-related harm of going to prison by keeping people out of prison—except when they're sending people to prison," said Delaney Ellison, a veteran Michigan harm reductionist and activist. "And that's exactly what drug courts do if you're resistant to treatment or broke. Poor, minority people can't afford to complete a time-consuming drug court regime. If a participant finds he can't pay the fines, go to four hours a day of outpatient treatment, and pay rent and buy food while trapped in the system, he finds a way to prioritize and abandons the drug court."

An adequate health care system that provides treatment on demand is what is needed, Ellison said. "And most importantly, when are we going to stop letting cops and lawyers—and this includes judges—regulate drugs?" he asked. "These people don't know anything about pharmacology. When do we lobby to let doctors and pharmacists regulate drugs?"

Drug Courts and Due Process Rights

Drug courts are also under attack on the grounds they deny due process rights to defendants. In Maryland, the state's public defender last week [in April 2009] argued that drug courts were unconstitutional, complaining that judges should not be allowed to send someone to jail repeatedly without a full judicial hearing.

"There is no due process in drug treatment court," Public Defender Nancy Forster told the Maryland Court of Appeals in a case that is yet to be decided.

Forster's argument aroused some interest from the appeals court judges. One of them, Judge Joseph Murphy, noted that a judge talking to one party in a case without the other party being present, which sometimes happens in drug courts, has raised due process concerns in other criminal proceedings. "Can you do that without violating the defendant's rights?" he asked.

A leading advocate of the position that drug courts interfere with due process rights is Williams College sociologist James Nolan. In an interview last year, Nolan summarized his problem with drug courts. "My concern is that if we make the law so concerned with being therapeutic, you forget about notions of justice such as proportionality of punishment, due process and the protection of individual rights," Nolan said. "Even though problem-solving advocates wouldn't want to do away with these things, they tend to fade into the background in terms of importance."

In that interview, Nolan cited a Miami-Dade County drug court participant forced to remain in the program for seven years. "So here, the goal is not about justice," he said. "The goal is to make someone well, and the consequences can be unjust because they are getting more of a punishment than they deserve."

Deutsch said he was "hesitant" to comment on criticisms of the drug court model, "but the fact of the matter is that when it comes to keeping drug addicted offenders out of the criminal justice system and in treatment, drug courts are the best option available."

For the Sentencing Project's King, drug courts are a step up from the depths of the punitive prohibitionist approach, but not much of one. "With the drug courts, we're in a better place now than we were 20 years ago, but it's not the place we want to be 20 years from now," he said. "The idea that some-body needs to enter the criminal justice system to access public drug treatment is a real tragedy."

Periodical and Internet Sources Bibliography

The following articles have been selected to supplement the diverse views presented in this chapter.

Radley Balko	"That Other War," *Reason*, January 11, 2010.
Economist	"How to Stop the Drug Wars," March 5, 2009.
Jens Glüsing	"Could Decriminalization Be the Answer?" *Spiegel Online*, February 10, 2010. www.spiegel.de.
NIDA Notes	"High-Risk Drug Offenders Do Better with Close Judicial Supervision," December 2008.
Roger Parloff	"How Marijuana Became Legal," *Fortune*, September 18, 2009.
Stanton Peele	"Drug Courts: You'd Think They Would Work," *Huffington Post*, June 22, 2010.
John H. Richardson	"A Radical Solution to End the Drug War: Legalize *Everything*," *Esquire*, September 1, 2009.
Phillip Smith	"Drug War a Devastating Failure, Scientists and Researchers Say in Vienna Declaration," *Drug War Chronicle*, July 9, 2010.
John Walters	"Our Drug Policy Is a Success," *Wall Street Journal*, December 5, 2008.
Michael Winerip	"Legalization? Now for the Hard Question," *New York Times*, May 15, 2009.
Ian Wishart	"The Truth About Marijuana Reform," *Investigate*, February 2010.
Rachel Godfrey Wood	"A Remarkable Failure," *New Internationalist*, June 2009.

For Further Discussion

Chapter 1

1. According to Monitoring the Future, some drug use by teenagers is down, but use for marijuana is up. Does this weaken its position? Use examples from the viewpoints to illustrate your response.

2. Maureen Martin and Joseph L. Bast argue that the dangers of smoking are exaggerated. In your opinion, does the National Cancer Institute distort the risks of smoking? Cite examples from the text to support your answer.

3. Do you agree or disagree with Maia Szalavitz that negative media reports on OxyContin influence doctors to prescribe their patients more dangerous prescription drugs instead? Why or why not?

Chapter 2

1. Michael Craig Miller argues that addiction is not a result of a person's flawed character but rather of distorted brain function. Do you agree or disagree with the author? Use examples from the viewpoint to support your reasoning.

2. Gene M. Heyman refutes the disease model of addiction. Does he successfully counter the claims of William L. White and Thomas McClellan, who support chemical dependency as a chronic condition? Why or why not?

Chapter 3

1. Robert John Araujo alleges that needle-exchange programs are immoral because drug abuse and HIV pose equal threats to society. Does Araujo offer a persuasive argument? Why or why not?

2. JoNel Aleccia writes that methadone is a powerful medication and deadly in the wrong hands. In your opinion, do the dangers she describes outweigh the benefits of methadone treatment to help with drug addiction? Cite examples from the viewpoints to illustrate your response.

3. Rachel Saslow warns that subjects who received doses of the experimental cocaine vaccine consumed much more of the drug to achieve a high. In your view, does Kayt Sukel address the dangers and downside of the cocaine vaccine satisfactorily? Why or why not?

Chapter 4

1. Joseph I. Cassilly maintains that crack cocaine is more destructive than powdered cocaine, but Bill Piper suggests that they are identical in effect. In your view, who provides the more compelling scientific evidence? Cite examples from the text to support your answer.

2. Phillip Smith does not support criminal sanctions in the treatment of addiction, but states that drug courts are better for addicts than prison. In your opinion, is Smith's position contradictory? Why or why not?

Organizations to Contact

The editors have compiled the following list of organizations concerned with the issues debated in this book. The descriptions are derived from materials provided by the organizations. All have publications or information available for interested readers. The list was compiled on the date of publication of the present volume; the information provided here may change. Be aware that many organizations take several weeks or longer to respond to inquiries, so allow as much time as possible.

Alcoholics Anonymous (AA)

PO Box 459, New York, NY   10163
(212) 870-3400
website: www.aa.org

Alcoholics Anonymous (AA) is a worldwide fellowship of sober alcoholics, whose recovery is based on twelve steps. AA requires no dues or fees, and the organization accepts no outside funds. It is self-supporting through voluntary contributions of members. It is not affiliated with any other organization. AA's primary purpose is to carry the AA message to the alcoholic who still suffers. Its publications include the books *Alcoholics Anonymous: Big Book* and *Twelve Steps and Twelve Traditions.*

American Council on Science and Health (ACSH)

1995 Broadway, 2nd Floor, New York, NY   10023-5860
(212) 362-7044 • fax: (212) 362-4919
e-mail: acsh@acsh.org
website: www.acsh.org

The American Council on Science and Health (ACSH) is a consumer education group concerned with issues related to food, nutrition, chemicals, pharmaceuticals, lifestyle, the environment, and health. It publishes booklets and articles such as *Health Effects of Menthol in Cigarettes* and "Smokeless Tobacco as Harm Reduction for Smokers."

Canadian Centre on Substance Abuse (CCSA)

75 Albert Street, Suite 500, Ottawa, ON   K1P 5E7
  Canada
(613) 235-4048 • fax: (613) 235-8101
e-mail: info@ccsa.ca
website: www.ccsa.ca

Established in 1988 by an act of the Canadian Parliament, the Canadian Centre on Substance Abuse (CCSA) works to mini-mize the harm associated with the use of alcohol, tobacco, and other drugs by sponsoring public debates on this issue. It dis-seminates information on the nature, extent, and consequences of substance abuse and supports organizations involved in substance abuse treatment, prevention, and educational pro-gramming.

Drug Policy Alliance (DPA)

70 West Thirty-sixth Street, 16th Floor, New York, NY   10018
(212) 613-8020 • fax: (212) 613-8021
e-mail: nyc@drugpolicy.org
website: www.drugpolicy.org

The Drug Policy Alliance (DPA) is an organization that pro-motes policy alternatives to the war on drugs. It is actively in-volved in the legislative process and seeks to roll back the ex-cesses of the drug war, block new initiatives viewed by the DPA as harmful, and promote sensible drug policy reforms. DPA's publications include *Preventing Overdose, Saving Lives* and *Safety First: A Reality-Based Approach to Teens and Drugs.*

Narcotics Anonymous (NA)

PO Box 9999, Van Nuys, CA   91409
(818) 773-9999 • fax: (818) 700-0700
website: www.na.org

Narcotics Anonymous, made up of more than eighteen thousand groups worldwide, is an organization of recovering drug addicts who meet regularly to help each other abstain from drugs. It publishes the monthly *NA Way Magazine* and annual conference reports.

**National Center on Addiction and Substance Abuse
at Columbia University (CASA)**
633 Third Avenue, 19th Floor, New York, NY   10017-6706
(212) 841-5200
website: www.casacolumbia.org

The National Center on Addiction and Substance Abuse at Columbia University (CASA) is a private, nonprofit organization that works to educate the public about the hazards of chemical dependency. The organization supports treatment as the best way to reduce chemical dependency. It produces publications describing the harmful effects of alcohol and drug addiction and effective ways to address the problem of substance abuse, including *How to Raise a Drug-Free Kid: The Straight Dope for Parents* and *High Society: How Substance Abuse Ravages America and What to Do About It*. CASA also publishes an annual report.

**National Council on Alcoholism and
Drug Dependence (NCADD)**
244 East Fifty-eighth Street, 4th Floor, New York, NY   10022
(212) 269-7797 • fax: (212) 269-7510
e-mail: national@ncadd.org
website: www.ncadd.org

The National Council on Alcoholism and Drug Dependence (NCADD) is a volunteer health organization that helps individuals overcome addictions; develops substance abuse prevention and education programs for youth; and advises the federal government on drug and alcohol policies. It operates the Campaign to Prevent Kids from Drinking, and its publications include brochures and fact sheets such as *Ask Dr. Bob: Questions and Answers on Alcoholism* and "Alcohol and Other Drugs in the Workplace."

National Institute on Alcohol Abuse and Alcoholism

5635 Fishers Lane, MSC 9304, Bethesda, MD   20892-9304
(301) 443-3860
e-mail: niaaaweb-r@exchange.nih.gov
website: www.niaaa.nih.gov

The National Institute on Alcohol Abuse and Alcoholism (NIAAA) supports and conducts biomedical and behavioral research on the causes, consequences, treatment, and prevention of alcoholism and alcohol-related problems. The institute disseminates the findings of this research to the public, researchers, policy makers, and health care providers. The NIAAA publishes a newsletter and publications for researchers and the public.

National Institute on Drug Abuse (NIDA)

6001 Executive Boulevard, Room 5213
Bethesda, MD   20892-9561
(301) 443-1124
e-mail: information@lists.nida.nih.gov
website: http://nida.nih.gov

The National Institute on Drug Abuse (NIDA) supports and conducts research on drug abuse—including the yearly Monitoring the Future survey—in order to improve addiction prevention, treatment, and policy efforts. It publishes the bimonthly *NIDA Notes* newsletter, the periodic *NIDA Fact Sheets*, and a catalog of research reports and public education materials such as *Inhalant Abuse* and *Cocaine: Abuse and Addiction*.

Office of National Drug Control Policy (ONDCP)

Drug Policy Information Clearinghouse
Rockville, MD   20849-6000
(800) 666-3332 • fax: (301) 519-5212
website: www.whitehousedrugpolicy.gov

The Office of National Drug Control Policy (ONDCP) formulates the government's national drug strategy and the president's antidrug policy, and it coordinates the federal agencies responsible for stopping drug trafficking. Its reports and fact sheets include "World Drug Report 2010" and "Laying a Foundation for Improving Public Health and Safety."

Rational Recovery
Box 800, Lotus, CA   95651
(530) 621-2667
website: https://rational.org

Rational Recovery is a national self-help organization that offers a cognitive rather than spiritual approach to recovery from alcoholism. Its philosophy holds that alcoholics can attain sobriety without depending on other people or a "higher power." It publishes materials including *The Small Book: A Revolutionary New Alternative* and *Rational Recovery: The New Cure for Substance Addiction.*

US Drug Enforcement Administration (DEA)
Mailstop: AES, 8701 Morrissette Drive, Springfield, VA   22152
(202) 307-1000
website: www.usdoj.gov/dea

The US Drug Enforcement Administration (DEA) is the federal agency charged with enforcing the nation's drug laws. The agency concentrates on stopping the smuggling and distribution of narcotics in the United States and abroad. Its website offers statistics on the drug war as well as provides speeches and congressional testimony concerning drug laws.

Bibliography of Books

A.J. Adams

Undrunk: A Skeptic's Guide to AA.
City Center, MN: Hazelden
Publishing, 2009.

Olivier Ameisen

The End of My Addiction. New York:
Farrar, Straus and Giroux, 2009.

Lisa C. Berry

Inside the Methadone Clinic Industry:
The Financial Exploitation of
America's Opiate Addicts. Tucson, AZ:
Wheatmark, 2007.

Joseph A.
Califano Jr.

High Society: How Substance Abuse
Ravages America and What to Do
About It. New York: PublicAffairs,
2007.

Howard Campbell

Drug War Zone: Frontline Dispatches
from the Streets of El Paso and Juárez.
Austin, TX: University of Texas Press,
2009.

Vanda
Febab-Brown

Shooting Up: Counterinsurgency and
the War on Drugs. Washington, DC:
Brookings Institution Press, 2010.

Richard Fields

Drugs in Perspective: Causes,
Assessment, Family, Prevention,
Intervention, and Treatment. 7th ed.
Boston, MA: McGraw-Hill, 2010.

Suzanne Fraser
and Kylie
Valentine

Substance and Substitution:
Methadone Subjects in Liberal
Societies. New York: Palgrave
Macmillan, 2008.

Paul Gootenberg — *Andean Cocaine: The Making of a Global Drug*. Chapel Hill, NC: University of North Carolina Press, 2008.

Gene M. Heyman — *Addiction: A Disorder of Choice*. Cambridge, MA: Harvard University Press, 2009.

John Hoffman and Susan Froemke, eds. — *Addiction: Why Can't They Just Stop? New Knowledge, New Treatments, New Hope*. New York: Rodale, 2007.

Darryl S. Ibana and William E. Cohen — *Uppers, Downers, All Arounders: Physical and Mental Effects of Psychoactive Drugs*. 6th ed. Medford, OR: CNS Productions, 2007.

Edward J. Khantzian and Mark J. Albanese — *Understanding Addiction as Self Medication: Finding Hope Behind the Pain*. Lanham, MD: Rowman & Littlefield, 2008.

Jean Kinney — *Loosening the Grip: A Handbook of Alcohol Information*. 9th ed. Boston, MA: McGraw-Hill, 2009.

Tara Koellhoffer — *Ecstasy and Other Club Drugs*. New York: Chelsea House Publishers, 2008.

Cynthia Kuhn, Scott Swartzwelder, and Wilkie Wilson — *Buzzed: The Straight Facts About the Most Used and Abused Drugs from Alcohol to Ecstasy*. 3rd ed. New York: W.W. Norton, 2008.

Deborah McCloskey and Barbara Sinor — *Addiction—What's Really Going On? Inside a Heroin Treatment Program.* Ann Arbor, MI: Love Healing Press, 2009.

William Cope Moyers — *Broken: My Story of Addiction and Redemption.* New York: Viking, 2006.

Julie O'Toole — *Heroin: A True Story of Drug Addiction, Hope, and Triumph.* Dunshaughlin, Ireland: Maverick House, 2005.

Frank Owen — *No Speed Limit: The Highs and Lows of Meth.* New York: St. Martin's Press, 2007.

Tim Pilcher — *E, the Incredibly Strange History of Ecstasy.* Philadelphia, PA: Running Press, 2008.

Doris Marie Provine — *Unequal Under Law: Race in the War on Drugs.* Chicago, IL: University of Chicago Press, 2007.

Jeri D. Ropero-Miller and Bruce A. Goldberger, eds. — *Handbook of Workplace Drug Testing.* 2nd ed. Washington, DC: American Association for Clinical Chemistry, 2009.

David Sheff — *Beautiful Boy: A Father's Journey Through His Son's Addiction.* Boston, MA: Houghton Mifflin, 2008.

Douglas Valentine — *The Strength of the Wolf: The Secret History of America's War on Drugs.* New York: Verso, 2006.

Index

A

Acamprosate, 73
Accreditation of drug courts, 174–175
Acetaldehyde, 96–97
ACLU, 163, 164
Acute care model for addiction, 79–81, 82
Adderall, 29, 57
   See also Stimulants
Addiction
   acute care model, 79–81, 82
   chronic disease model, 75–88, 121, 122, 127, 180
   costs, 72
   defined, 54
   environmental factors, 94–99
   genetic factors, 73, 81, 92, 94–99
   incentives against, 90, 92–93
   is a brain disease, 71–74
   is not a disease, 89–93
   morality, 113–119, 126, 127, 180
   as self-medication, 69–70
   stigma, 126, 127
   sustained recovery management model, 80–81, 82, 85–88
   See also Drug treatment and prevention programs; Recovery; Vaccines
Addiction: A Disorder of Choice (Heyman), 90
Adinoff, Bryon, 69–70
African Americans
   marijuana arrests, 15, 16
   prisoner population, 163
   sentencing disparities for crack and powder cocaine, 153, 158, 162–163
AIDS. *See* HIV
Aiken, Sally, 132
Akst, Daniel, 89–93
Albanese, Mark J., 69
Albany Catholic Charities, 112–119
Alcohol
   binge drinking, 32
   driving-while-impaired (DWI) courts, 171
   methadone treatment, 124
   teen use, 22, 32–33
   tolerance, 96
Alcoholism
   chronic disease model, 78, 93
   naltrexone treatment, 72, 97–99
   ondansetron treatment, 73
   treatment history, 78–80
Aleccia, JoNel, 130–137
Allen, Ron, 16
Alprazolam. *See* Benzodiazepines
Amantadine, 124
American Cancer Society, 37
American Civil Liberties Union, 163, 164
Amphetamines, teen abuse, 29, 57, 60
Anabolic steroids. *See* Steroid abuse
Antabuse, 147
Anti-smoking groups, criticism of, 42–51